Sharon O'Connor's Menus and Music

Lighthearted Gourmet

Recipes for Lighter, Healthier Dinners

Romantic Solo Piano Music

OTHER BOOKS IN THE MENUS AND MUSIC SERIES

Sharon O'Connor's Menus and Music

Lighthearted Gourmet

Recipes for Lighter, Healthier Dinners

Romantic Solo Piano Music

Menus and Music Productions, Inc.

Emeryville, California

Illustrations © 1994 Tom Kamegai

Library of Congress Cataloging-in-Publication Data
O'Connor, Sharon
Menus and Music Volume IX
Lighthearted Gourmet
Recipes for Lighter, Healthier Dinners
Romantic Solo Piano Music

Includes Index
1. Cookery 2. Entertaining
I. Title
95-077125

ISBN 1-883914-11-6 (paperback)
ISBN 1-883914-09-4 (hardcover)

Menus and Music is published by

Menus and Music Productions, Inc.
1462 66th Street
Emeryville, CA 94608
(510) 658-9100

Book and cover design by Michael Osborne Design, Inc.
Cover photograph by Paul Franz-Moore
Food styling by Amy Nathan
Drawings by Tom Kamegai

Manufactured in the United States of America
10 9 8 7 6 5 4 3 2 1

CONTENTS

INTRODUCTION

It is impossible to live pleasurably without living wisely,
well, and justly, and impossible to live wisely, well, and
justly without living pleasurably.

—Epicurus

Gracious dining at home creates a moment in the day that can provide pleasurable sustenance, contribute to a healthy lifestyle, and change our state of mind. Preparing and eating a dinner of lighter, healthier ingredients rich in flavor, freshness, color, and texture is an enjoyable way to promote health, and listening to beautiful music during dinner creates a realm of delight. When we feed our bodies with good food and our spirits with beautiful music, the potential for a great dining experience increases dramatically.

The recipes in this cookbook are not about deprivation or self-denial, nor is this a serious nonfat cookbook or diet book. It is, however, a text for those who wish to dine more lightly in a reasonable and enjoyable way. Twenty-four talented and creative chefs, each with his or her own distinct personality and style, provide a sampling of the wonderful cuisine that is now being served all over America. Their recipes call for ingredients that are fresh, pure and simple, and they have applied new creative culinary standards to lighter dining. Food is often grilled to maximize its flavor without adding fat or calories. Broiling, steaming, poaching, and baking are also commonly used techniques. More vegetables and leaner meats are featured, while the use of salt and dairy products is minimized. Vegetable- and fruit-based sauces, salsas, chutneys, spices, and fresh herbs add flair and enhance flavor. Fresh seasonal fruits are often showcased for dessert. The chefs have provided a wonderful array of recipes for you to cook at home.

These recipes will provide satisfying, tasty, and attractive dishes for quality dining. They have complex flavors and are so attractive and colorful that they will fill you up without weighing you down. This kind of food proves you don't have to choose between good taste and good health.

After all, if food isn't delicious, no matter how healthful it is, no one will want to eat it. Home cooks can create food that is just as good as that of professional chefs; you don't need to be a highly skilled cook to prepare any of these dishes. I hope this book will spark your creativity and increase your enjoyment of food rich in flavor, freshness, color, and texture.

In today's hectic world, music has an increasingly important role to play in the quality of our daily lives. Listening to beautiful music during dinner establishes a more human pace that encourages us to take the time to dine rather than just consume food. Medical studies show that dinner music causes people to eat less and to eat more slowly, aids digestion, and increases the enjoyment of food.

The melodic original music that pianist Dick Hindman recorded for this volume will create a peaceful mood and take you away from outside distractions. It has been fifteen years since I first heard this ingenious artist perform; his music captured my heart then and still does today. Each of these fifteen compositions is an intimate and reflective gem. Hindman knows how to create and perform *tunes*—how to harmonize them, set them, and phrase them like a singer. He is an unabashed romantic, and his passion for music speaks directly to the heart and soul.

This volume of *Menus and Music* celebrates lighter, healthier dining with beautiful music, two combined pleasures that will add to a healthier lifestyle. To your health and happiness! Enjoy!

—Sharon O'Connor

Introduction

MUSIC NOTES

Dick Hindman was trained as a classical pianist, but at this point in his career he's composing and performing music the way he wants to play it, not the way others expect him to play. For him, music is communication. If there were no one in the world to play for, Hindman says he might not touch the piano again.

> Music is to share. But I don't want to share a caricature of myself. I want to share the way that I really feel, because when people respond to that, there is a significant diminishing of the sense of aloneness we all feel. There isn't just applause, but a sense of communion. I reveal something of myself to you, and you say yes, I feel that too—then we have a real sense of communion. And if I don't take the chance of revealing myself, I may get you to applaud, I may get you to agree I'm really good, but I'm still alone because I haven't really let you touch me; you're just responding to whatever mask I wanted to show.

Hindman reveals himself in the inventive original music he composes and performs here; I admire his courage and his artistry.

A Sailor Looks at the Stars

This piece evokes a feeling of relaxation and profound calm. When he composed the piece, Hindman had in his mind the image of a big three-masted sailing ship of long ago. The ship is on a beautiful sea on a quiet, warm night. The sailor is standing all alone on the deck. He's on watch, looking up at the star-filled sky. The boat gently rocks, and the sailor can faintly hear the sound of the waves. It is a timeless moment when he looks at things from the perspective of eternity and experiences a feeling of tremendous peace and acceptance.

And When We Say Goodbye

The title fits the opening phrase of a lovely melody that is a tribute to Michel Legrand. Hindman says he hears the ballad with lyrics by Marilyn and Alan Bergman: "something really great and poetic and depressing."

Ballad in G Minor

The alluring motivic melody of this abstract ballad was a favorite of Stan Getz.

Bossa Nova Nights

This piece evokes a tropical Brazilian evening with romance in the air. When writing it, Hindman had the wonderful composer Antonio Carlos Jobim in mind as well as the memory of performing "The Girl from Ipanema" with Stan Getz. Hindman reaches into his musical unconscious and we are swept away on a voyage to a tropical world of palm trees, trade winds, and moonlight on the water.

Broadway Tune

A slightly wry tip of the hat to the type of songs heard in overblown Broadway musicals. This tune highlights Hindman's ability to play melodic lines on the piano as if he were singing them.

The Face of Love to Come

A gorgeous rhapsody about someone who is looking for love in the future, not knowing who that person will be or how he or she will look, but hoping that someone is waiting for them somewhere.

Flying

This song was written for the bird Gonzo, one of Jim Hensen's Muppets. Gonzo can't fly; he sees the other birds flying around, but he's stuck on the ground. He needs someone to come along and show him how to do it, or just to believe in him and give him the courage to try. This lovely song is about anybody who wants to fly and isn't quite sure yet that they can.

Music Notes

Flying

I wish that I knew how to fly,
Winging and soaring on high,
But it seems so far up
From down here on the ground
That I don't have the courage to try.

Why should it be, there's only me
Down here where no one can see?
If it takes me forever
I'll get it together.
I'll learn how, and then I'll be free.

I'll go higher, and still higher,
As high as any balloon.
I'll keep climbing and keep reaching
Until I'm touching the moon.

Maybe someday, somebody may
Take time to show me the way.
Then I'll take off and soar,
That's what God made me for,
And I'll softly go flying away.

Lost in a Dream

A delicate love song in which being lost in a dream at first has the connotation of feeling trapped or vulnerable. By the end of the song, the idea of being lost in a dream has become the lovely sensation of being lost in a dream of love.

Music Notes

Movie Theme

A weirdly stretching sort of melody influenced by Bach—in particular, the Siciliano from the Sonata for Flute and Harpsichord in $E^\flat$ minor. Although the melody is very beautiful, it is composed of a series of strange intervals.

Odiyan

This piece was composed for the opening ceremony of Odiyan, a magnificent center built by Tarthang Tulka for the preservation of Tibetan culture and Tibetan Buddhism in Sonoma County, California. Hindman studied with Tarthang Tulka at the Nyingma Institute in Berkeley and was asked to compose and perform some music for the new center.

Paris

A French-style song inspired by being driven through the streets of Paris in the springtime and seeing the tops of buildings and trees float by in a dreamlike fashion.

Sandy's Theme

A song composed for a friend. The melody has a repeating motif and is a salute to the music of Jerome Kern.

The Turning Song

A captivating song about the giddiness of falling in love. Hindman hears it as the soundtrack for a scene in a romantic Broadway musical. Two people have just fallen in love and are feeling dizzy because their world is suddenly turning and spinning.

Strange Interval Waltz

This remarkable tune has an old-fashioned feeling, but with a sense of dislocation. Hindman was thinking of traditional waltzes, like the kind his grandparents enjoyed, seen through the eyes of Prokofiev.

Music Notes

We Belong Together

A particularly fine performance of a romantic ballad about the joy of true love. This song is for lovers who believe that they belong together and that their love will grow ever stronger with time.

Dick Hindman is a recording artist, composer, arranger, accompanist, and jazz clinician. He has shared the stage with such artists as Stan Getz, Sonny Stitt, Richie Cole, Manhattan Transfer, Clark Terry, Sonny Stitt, and Shelley Manne, to name only a few, and has toured the North American continent, Europe, and Japan.

THE SCIENCE OF DINING AND MUSIC

The style of music played in a dining room affects the eating habits of the diners, according to Johns Hopkins researchers at the Health, Weight, and Stress Clinic of the Good Samaritan Hospital in Baltimore. Research at the clinic shows that diners listening to fast, loud music eat more than those listening to slow, calm music. Soothing dinner music also caused participants to eat smaller portions, consume fewer forkfuls per minute, chew their food more thoroughly, and have longer conversations with each other.

When dining without music, the study participants ate at a rate of 3.9 bites per minute and finished eating in about forty minutes, and one third of them requested second helpings. When dining with slow, restful background music, the bites per minute decreased to 3.2, the bite size became smaller, no one asked for seconds, and most participants left a quarter of the food on their plates.

Listening to slow, soothing music during meals resulted in fewer digestive complaints as well as reports that the food tasted better. Researchers attribute this to slower chewing, which allows subjects to smell their food better. Chewing forces air from the throat to the nose, thereby increasing the sense of smell. Since aroma is strongly linked to the sense of taste, a heightened ability to detect it through slower chewing and swallowing makes food more flavorful, according to a report in the Tufts University *Diet and Nutrition Letter*.

Playing music softly rather than at loud volume during meals may also affect diners: Recent studies show that loud dinner music results in more food being consumed. The Lempert Report of Belleville, New Jersey concludes that by choosing soft, soothing music, people on a low-fat diet may increase their weight loss by at least five pounds a month.

No matter how conclusive such research may be, it is undeniable that dining with beautiful music adds to the gracious enjoyment of good food.

THE NUTRITIONAL DATA

The nutritional composition of each of the recipes in this cookbook was calculated by registered dietitian Karen Duester at the Food Consulting Company of San Diego, California.

When a recipe gives a choice of ingredients, the first choice was the one used to determine the nutritional data. Optional ingredients and those listed without a specific quantity (such as salt and pepper to taste) were not included in the calculations. When a range of ingredient amounts or serving sizes is given, the smaller amount or portion was used to calculate the nutritional data.

The Nutritional Data

Brava Terrace

St. Helena, California

Chef-proprietor Fred Halpert focuses on what he calls "cuisines of the sun" at his wine-country bistro in California's Napa Valley. Inspired by the wine-country cooking of France, Italy, and especially California, Halpert's skills were learned at the elbows of some of the world's most respected chefs. A Florida native, he has worked and studied with Michelin three-star chefs Roger Verge, Alain Senderens, and Alain Chapel. The desire for a restaurant of his own and his love of the Napa Valley, which reminds him of Southern France, led him to open Brava Terrace, just north of St. Helena, in 1990.

Brava Terrace's comfortable, casual dining room is light and airy, with a whitewashed ceiling, exposed wood beams, a large stone fireplace, and an open kitchen. Lovely outdoor terraces and a heated enclosed deck offer spectacular views of vineyards and Howell Mountain. The menu relies heavily on "fresh herbs, garlic, tomatoes, olive oil, and seafood," says Halpert. "Provençal cooking doesn't mask flavors—it opens up possibilities for matching food with the abundant flavors of Napa Valley wines." Halpert personally selects all the wines on his focused list, which includes special selections from his Napa Valley neighbors and has received *The Wine Spectator's* Award of Excellence. Tuesday nights Brava Terrace features Ribs and Zin, with Halpert's own barbecue sauce and Napa Valley Zinfandels by the tumbler.

Brava Terrace

THE MENU
Brava Terrace

Spicy Peppered Oysters with Romesco Sauce

Cassoulet of Green Lentils with Lamb, Sausage, and Pork

Pan-roasted Pippin Apples and Pistachio Butter

Serves Four

Spicy Peppered Oysters with Romesco Sauce

8 oysters in the shell
½ cup unbleached all-purpose flour
½ cup dried bread crumbs
Salt to taste
¼ teaspoon cayenne pepper
¼ teaspoon freshly ground black pepper, plus more for garnish
1 egg
Canola oil for deep-frying
Romesco Sauce (recipe follows)

Shuck the oysters, severing the muscle from the shell. Discard the shallow half shells, retaining the deeper shells to serve the oysters.

Place the flour and bread crumbs in separate shallow bowls and season *each* with salt, ⅛ teaspoon of the cayenne, and ⅛ teaspoon of the black pepper. Blend each mixture well. Beat the egg well in a shallow bowl. Dredge the oysters in the seasoned flour, dip in the beaten egg, and dredge them in the seasoned bread crumbs.

To a large, heavy skillet, add canola oil to a depth of 2 inches. Heat over high heat until almost smoking. Lower the heat slightly and deep-fry the oysters until brown. Remove the oysters with a slotted spoon and drain on paper towels. Place some romesco sauce in each oyster shell and top with a fried oyster and a grind of black pepper.

Makes 4 servings

Per Serving (without romesco sauce)
Calories 350 • Carbohydrates 16 g • Cholesterol 105 mg
Fat 26 g • Protein 13 g • Sodium 230 mg

Romesco Sauce

½ red bell pepper, roasted, peeled and seeded (see page 232)

1 or 2 garlic cloves

1 tomato, peeled and seeded (see page 231)

3 tablespoons blanched almonds

¼ teaspoon red pepper flakes

¼ teaspoon salt

¼ teaspoon ground black pepper

½ cup extra-virgin olive oil

3 tablespoons balsamic vinegar

In blender or food processor, purée the bell pepper, garlic, tomato, almonds, pepper flakes, salt, and pepper until smooth. With the motor running, slowly add the olive oil and the vinegar; the romesco sauce will emulsify and become fairly thick. Store in an airtight container in the refrigerator.

Makes about 1 cup

Per Serving
Calories 70 • Carbohydrates 1 g • Cholesterol 0 mg
Fat 8 g • Protein less than 1 g • Sodium 35 mg

Brava Terrace

Cassoulet of Green Lentils with Lamb, Sausage, and Pork

2 tablespoons olive oil

½ onion, diced

½ carrot, peeled and diced

1 celery stalk, diced

1 cup French green lentils (available in some supermarkets and
  specialty foods markets)

1 bay leaf

1 fresh thyme sprig

⅔ cup chicken stock (see page 225) or canned low-salt chicken broth

8 ounces boneless leg of lamb, trimmed of all fat

8 ounces boneless pork loin

Salt and ground white pepper to taste

8 ounces fresh turkey, venison, or chicken sausage (available in some
  supermarkets and specialty foods markets)

1 tablespoon unsalted butter

8 ounces mushrooms, quartered

½ cup veal stock (see page 227)

Minced fresh chives for garnish

In a large, heavy pot over medium heat, heat 1 tablespoon of the olive oil and sauté the onion, carrot, and celery until tender, about 7 minutes. Add the lentils, bay leaf, and thyme and sauté for 1 minute.

Raise the heat to high, add the stock or broth, and bring the liquid to a boil. Reduce the heat to medium, cover, and cook, stirring occasionally, for 15 minutes, or until the lentils are firm but tender.

Cut the lamb and pork loin in half and season with salt and pepper. In a large skillet over high heat, heat the remaining 1 tablespoon olive oil and brown the lamb and pork on all sides. Remove from the pan and set aside. In the same pan, brown the sausages on all sides. Quarter the lamb and

Brava Terrace

pork pieces and cut the sausages in half.

In a large skillet or sauté pan over medium heat, melt the butter and sauté the mushrooms for 2 or 3 minutes.

Return the lentils to medium heat and add the lamb, pork, sausage meats, and veal stock. Cook for 2 minutes for rare meat, 4 minutes for medium meat, and 6 minutes for well-done meat. Divide the cassoulet among 4 serving bowls and garnish with chives.

Makes 4 servings

Per Serving
Calories 550 • Carbohydrates 33 g • Cholesterol 115 mg
Fat 26 g • Protein 48 g • Sodium 520 mg

Pan-roasted Pippin Apples with Pistachio Butter

Pistachio Butter
¾ cup pistachios
⅓ cup unsalted butter at room temperature
⅓ cup granulated sugar

4 Pippin apples
2 tablespoons unsalted butter
3 tablespoons plus ⅓ cup granulated sugar
2 cups water
1 cinnamon stick
Vanilla ice cream or frozen yogurt for serving
Sifted confectioners' sugar for garnish
Chocolate shavings for garnish
4 fresh mint sprigs for garnish

Preheat the oven to 350°F. To make the pistachio butter: Spread the pistachios on a baking sheet and bake for 3 to 5 minutes, or until lightly toasted. Pour the nuts into a colander, let cool, then shake the colander over the sink to discard some of the peels. In a blender or food processor, blend the pistachios with the butter and sugar until smooth; set aside.

Using a sharp knife, slice 2 of the apples in half crosswise and remove the cores. In a large skillet or sauté pan over medium-high heat, cook the butter until it is just beginning to brown and sauté the apple halves until lightly browned. Remove from heat and sprinkle with the 3 tablespoons sugar. Place the apples in an ovenproof dish and bake in the preheated oven for 8 to 10 minutes, or until the apples are tender when pierced with a fork. Fill the halved apples with the pistachio butter, return to the oven, and bake for 1 minute. Set aside.

In a medium saucepan over high heat, bring the ⅓ cup sugar, the water, and cinnamon stick to a boil and cook until the sugar is thoroughly dissolved.

Brava Terrace

Slice the remaining 2 apples ⅛ inch thick. Add the apple slices to the cinnamon water and simmer until the apples are tender. Using a slotted spoon, remove the apple slices and divide them evenly among 4 shallow bowls. Place a hot apple half on top of each bed of sliced apples. Top with a spoonful of vanilla ice cream or frozen yogurt. Garnish with powdered sugar, chocolate shavings, and a mint sprig; serve immediately.

Makes 4 servings

Per Serving (Without ice cream, frozen yogurt, or garnishes)
Calories 520 • Carbohydrates 57 g • Cholesterol 55 mg
Fat 33 g • Protein 5 g • Sodium 5 mg

Cafe Allegro

Kansas City, Missouri

Stephen Cole realized a long-held dream when he opened Cafe Allegro just north of Westport, a revitalized neighborhood in Kansas City. Since its opening in 1984, the restaurant has garnered outstanding critical acclaim and national recognition that includes a first-place ranking in Kansas City's *Zagat Restaurant Survey* in 1995, and the prestigious DiRoNa Award each year since 1992. In addition to his work at Cafe Allegro, chef Cole donates his talents to efforts that raise money for hunger relief and the homeless and is active in professional chefs' organizations.

The innovative seasonal menu blends influences from France, Italy, Asia, and America. Two dining rooms provide a welcoming atmosphere and are highlighted by frequently changing art exhibitions by local artists. An extensive wine list complements the cross-cultural menu. The following recipes were created by chefs Stephen Cole and Stu Stein.

THE MENU
Cafe Allegro

Seared Scallops Wrapped in Leeks with Citrus Vinaigrette

Black Bean Soup with Smoked Chicken and Pico de Gallo

Salmon Paillards with Crisp Noodle Cakes and Cilantro-Ginger Sauce

Pear and Walnut Soufflé

Serves Four

Seared Scallops Wrapped in Leeks with Citrus Vinaigrette

4 large sea scallops

4 tender inner leek leaves, green part only

Kosher salt to taste

2 teaspoons peanut oil

½ cup Citrus Vinaigrette (recipe follows)

Mixed baby greens for garnish

Blanch the leek leaves in boiling salted water, about 2 minutes; drain on paper towels. Wrap 1 leaf around the circumference of each scallop and secure with a toothpick. Pat the scallops dry with paper towels and sprinkle them with salt on both sides.

In a cast-iron skillet or on a griddle over high heat, heat the peanut oil until almost smoking. Sauté the scallops on both sides until browned, about 1 minute on each side.

Place 1 scallop in the center of each of 4 plates and drizzle 2 table-spoons of the citrus vinaigrette over each scallop. Garnish each plate with a few baby greens and serve at once.

Makes 4 first-course servings

Per Serving (without mixed baby greens)
Calories 150 • Carbohydrates 5 g • Cholesterol 5 mg
Fat 13 g • Protein 4 g • Sodium 320 mg

Citrus Vinaigrette

1 lime
1 lemon
½ grapefruit
1 orange
¾ cup extra-virgin olive oil
1½ tablespoons sherry vinegar
2 tablespoons soy sauce
Pinch of cayenne pepper
¼ teaspoon celery salt
Dash of Tabasco sauce
15 pink peppercorns, lightly crushed
2 teaspoons grated peeled fresh ginger
2 tablespoons minced fresh cilantro
½ teaspoon kosher salt
¼ teaspoon freshly ground black pepper

Peel, section (see page 232), and roughly chop the lime, lemon, grape-fruit half, and orange, retaining all of the juices. Set aside.

In a blender or food processor, blend the olive oil, vinegar, soy sauce, cayenne, celery salt, and Tabasco. Add the fruits and juices and all the remaining ingredients. Blend until just incorporated. Cover and refrigerate the vinaigrette until chilled.

Makes about 2 cups

Per Serving
Calories 50 • Carbohydrates 2 g • Cholesterol 0 mg
Fat 5 g • Protein 0 g • Sodium 110 mg

Black Bean Soup with Smoked Chicken and Pico de Gallo

1 cup dried black beans

4 cups water

1 bay leaf

3 garlic cloves

2 cups ½-inch-thick onion slices

2 zucchini, cut lengthwise into ½-inch-thick slices

1 whole chicken breast, boned

2 tablespoons canola oil

1 tablespoon dried thyme

1 cup finely diced peeled carrots

2 cups finely diced celery

1 cup dry red wine

2 tablespoons dried basil

1 tablespoon Worcestershire sauce

1 teaspoon liquid smoke (optional)

1 teaspoon green Tabasco sauce

4 cups chicken stock (see page 225) or canned low-salt chicken broth

¼ cup Pico de Gallo (recipe follows)

Rinse and pick through the beans. Place them in a bowl, cover with cold water, and soak overnight; drain. In a large saucepan, combine the beans, 4 cups water, bay leaf, and 2 of the garlic cloves and bring to a boil. Reduce the heat to low and simmer for 30 to 40 minutes, or until the beans are tender.

Light a fire in a charcoal grill. While the coals are heating, mince the remaining garlic clove. In a medium bowl, toss together the onions, zucchini, chicken, 1 tablespoon of the canola oil, the thyme, and minced garlic and set aside at room temperature.

When the coals are hot, grill the onions, zucchini, and chicken until the vegetables are lightly charred and the chicken is opaque throughout. Set the chicken aside and cut the onions and zucchini into dice.

In a large saucepan over medium-low heat, heat the remaining 1 table-spoon oil and sauté the carrots, celery, and diced onions and zucchini for 2 or 3 minutes. Cover and cook for 5 minutes. Remove the lid and add the wine, basil, Worcestershire sauce, optional liquid smoke, green Tabasco, stock or broth, and black beans. Simmer for 30 minutes, or until the soup is the desired consistency.

Thinly slice the grilled chicken breast. Ladle the soup into 4 shallow bowls and top with some chicken strips and pico de gallo.

Makes 4 to 6 servings

Per Serving
Calories 260 • Carbohydrates 32 g • Cholesterol 15 mg
Fat 7 g • Protein 15 g • Sodium 120 mg

Pico de Gallo

1 tomato, seeded and diced
½ jalapeño chili, seeded and minced
½ onion, finely diced
¼ cup minced fresh cilantro
Juice of ½ fresh lime
Salt and freshly ground black pepper to taste

In a small glass or ceramic bowl, combine all of the ingredients, cover, and chill in the refrigerator.

Makes about 1 cup

Per Serving
Calories 5 • Carbohydrates 1 g • Cholesterol 0 mg
Fat 0 g • Protein 0 g • Sodium 0 mg

Cafe Allegro

Salmon Paillards with Crisp Noodle Cakes and Cilantro-Ginger Sauce

8 thin salmon fillet slices (3 ounces each)
1 tablespoon canola oil for coating

Crisp Noodle Cakes
8 ounces Chinese dried wheat vermicelli (available in Asian markets)
2 teaspoons canola oil
1 tablespoon Asian sesame oil
4 green onions, with tops, sliced into shreds

Salt and freshly ground black pepper to taste
Cilantro-Ginger Sauce (recipe follows)

Place a large piece of waxed paper or parchment paper on a flat work surface. Coat each slice of salmon lightly with canola oil and place on the paper. Cover the salmon slices with a second large piece of waxed paper or parchment paper. With the flat side of a meat mallet or the bottom of a large bottle, lightly pound the slices until they are about ½ inch thick. Transfer the salmon slices to a platter, cover, and chill in the refrigerator until ready to serve.

To make the crisp noodle cakes: In a large pot of boiling salted water, cook the vermicelli according to package directions until tender. Drain and rinse with cold water.

In a medium bowl, toss the noodles with 1 teaspoon of the canola oil. Drizzle in the sesame oil, add the green onions, and toss to combine. Cover and refrigerate the noodles until chilled.

Just before serving, in a nonstick 6-inch skillet over high heat, heat the remaining 1 teaspoon canola oil until almost smoking. Add about 1½ cups of the noodles and press them into a cake with a metal spatula; cook until golden, turn, and cook on the other side until golden. Transfer the cake to a plate and keep warm in a low oven. Repeat to make 4 noodle cakes.

Heat a large skillet or griddle over high heat until very hot. Season the salmon paillards with salt and pepper. Working quickly, place the salmon in the pan or on the griddle and sear until just opaque, turn, and sear until just opaque on the second side.

Arrange the salmon slices on top of the crisp noodle cakes, spoon a little of the cilantro-ginger sauce over, and serve at once.

Makes 4 servings

Per Serving (without cilantro-ginger sauce)
Calories 550 • Carbohydrates 45 g • Cholesterol 75 mg
Fat 20 g • Protein 44 g • Sodium 80 mg

Cilantro-Ginger Sauce

½ tablespoon minced garlic
1½ tablespoons minced peeled fresh ginger
¼ teaspoon red pepper flakes
1 serrano or red Fresno or Anaheim chili, seeded and minced
½ tablespoon sugar
⅓ cup minced pickled ginger (available in Asian markets)
¼ teaspoon kosher salt
½ cup packed fresh cilantro sprigs
½ tablespoon Asian sesame oil
2 tablespoons distilled white vinegar
½ tablespoon unseasoned rice vinegar
½ cup canola oil

In a blender or food processor, blend the garlic, ginger, pepper flakes, chili, sugar, pickled ginger, salt, cilantro, and sesame oil. Briefly blend in the white vinegar and rice vinegar. With the motor running, add the canola oil in a thin stream until the sauce thickens. Chill in the refrigerator until ready to use.

Makes about ¾ cup

Per Serving
Calories 90 • Carbohydrates 1 g • Cholesterol 0 mg
Fat 10 g • Protein 0 g • Sodium 55 mg

Pear and Walnut Soufflé

½ cup sugar
½ cup water
4 Anjou pears, peeled, cored, and halved
Grated zest of ½ lemon
1 tablespoon cornstarch or arrowroot
Juice of ½ lemon
⅛ cup Poire William or other pear eau-de-vie
8 large egg whites
Pinch of salt
¼ cup walnut pieces, toasted (see page 232)
Sifted confectioners' sugar for dusting

Preheat the oven to 400°F. Lightly rub four ½-cup soufflé dishes or ramekins with unsalted butter and coat with sugar.

In a large saucepan over high heat, combine the sugar and water and cook until the sugar dissolves. Reduce the heat to medium-low, add the pears, and simmer until the pears are tender. Remove the pears with a slotted spoon and reserve the sugar syrup. Let the pears cool.

Dice half of the pears and reserve them. In a blender or food processor, purée the remaining pears and the lemon zest. In a large saucepan over medium heat, combine the pear purée and reserved sugar syrup and simmer until the liquid reduces to 2 cups, about 20 minutes.

In a small bowl, stir together the cornstarch or arrowroot and lemon juice until well blended. Stir the cornstarch mixture into the simmering pear purée and cook until thick, about 2 minutes. Remove from heat and stir in the pear eau-de-vie.

Preheat the oven to 400°F. In a large bowl, beat the egg whites with a pinch of salt until soft peaks form. Gently fold the whites into the pear mixture.

Place an equal amount of the reserved diced pears and the walnuts in the center of each prepared soufflé dish or ramekin. Spoon in the pear purée and smooth the tops with a rubber spatula. Place the soufflés on the lowest shelf of the oven and cook until puffed and golden, about 20 minutes. Dust with confectioners' sugar and serve immediately.

Makes 4 servings

Per Serving
Calories 340 • Carbohydrates 65 g • Cholesterol 0 mg
Fat 6 g • Protein 9 g • Sodium 150 mg

Carbo's Cafe

Atlanta, Georgia

Carmen and Bob Mazurek opened Carbo's Cafe in 1980 with the intention of creating a dining experience unlike any other in Atlanta. Their constant refinements and additions to their restaurant-supper club include the completion of an upstairs Grand Ballroom in 1987. A re-creation of a classic grand ballroom with eighteen-foot ceilings and period architectural detailing, the room offers an elegant space for private parties, reception banquets, business meetings, and weddings. Smaller private dining rooms have also been added, and a lovely sidewalk cafe provides an ideal setting for outdoor dining. Carbo's mahogany-paneled piano bar is a favorite spot for enjoying nightly performances.

Outstanding American-Continental cuisine, an award-winning wine list, elegant decor, and attentive serice have earned Carbo's Cafe a Three-Star Award from the Mobil Travel Guide. The following menu and recipes were created by chef Jon Toler.

THE MENU
Carbo's Cafe

𝄢

Grilled Vidalia Onions with Yellow Tomato Essence

Field Greens Salad with Black Pepper Vinaigrette

*Peppercorn-encrusted Roast Pork Tenderloin with Georgia Chutney and
Buttermilk Mashed Potatoes*

Genoise with Blackberry Compote and Yogurt Crème Frâiche

Serves Four

Grilled Vidalia Onions with Yellow Tomato Essence

2 young Vidalia or other sweet white onions (6 to 8 ounces each)
1½ teaspoons salt, plus more to taste
¼ teaspoon ground white pepper, plus more to taste
2 yellow or red tomatoes
4 teaspoons apple cider vinegar
1 basil leaf
½ cup canola oil
1 small head radicchio, cut into fine shreds
Minced fresh chives for garnish

Light a fire in a charcoal grill. Preheat the oven to 400°F. Using a sharp knife, slice two thirds off the top of each onion, and split the onions in half crosswise. Season with the 1½ teaspoons salt and ¼ teaspoon pepper; set aside for 5 minutes at room temperature.

Place the onions cut-side down on an oiled heated cooking rack over hot coals and cook for 1½ minutes. Give the onions a quarter turn and cook for an additional 1½ minutes. Remove the onions from the grill, place in an ovenproof pan, and bake in the preheated oven for 5 minutes, or until tender. Set aside.

In a blender or food processor, blend the tomatoes, vinegar, and basil leaf until smooth. Strain through a fine-meshed sieve. Rinse out the blender or food processor and add the tomato mixture. With the motor running, slowly pour the canola oil into the tomato mixture until emulsified. Season with salt and pepper.

In the center of each of 4 plates, mound some of the radicchio and place an onion on top with the grill marks showing. Drizzle some of the tomato essence around the perimeter of the plate and sprinkle with the chives.

Makes 4 servings

Per Serving
Calories 300 • Carbohydrates 12 g • Cholesterol 0 mg
Fat 28 g • Protein 2 g • Sodium 820 mg

37

Field Greens Salad with Black Pepper Vinaigrette

Black Pepper Vinaigrette

3 tablespoons sugar

3 tablespoons unseasoned rice wine vinegar

¾ teaspoon freshly ground black pepper

6 tablespoons canola oil

2 tablespoons chopped pecans

1 tablespoon sugar

4 handfuls mixed baby greens

2 tablespoons finely chopped green onion

4 strawberries, diced, plus 4 strawberries, halved lengthwise, for garnish

To make the vinaigrette: In a small saucepan over low heat, combine the sugar, vinegar, and pepper and cook until the sugar is dissolved. Whisk in the canola oil in a thin stream until emulsified. Set aside and let cool.

Preheat the oven to 400°F. Moisten the pecans with water and roll them in the sugar to coat. Place them on a baking pan and bake in the preheated oven for 10 minutes, or until the sugar caramelizes; set aside to cool.

In a large bowl, toss together the baby greens, vinaigrette, pecans, green onion, and diced strawberries. Divide evenly among 4 plates and garnish with the halved strawberries.

Makes 4 servings

Per Serving

Calories 280 • Carbohydrates 19 g • Cholesterol 0 mg

Fat 23 g • Protein 1 g • Sodium 15 mg

Peppercorn-encrusted Roast Pork Tenderloin with Georgia Chutney and Buttermilk Mashed Potatoes

Two 12-ounce pork tenderloins (silver skin and fat removed)
4 teaspoons salt, plus more to taste
½ cup cracked black pepper
20 green beans
Freshly ground black pepper to taste
Buttermilk Mashed Potatoes (recipe follows)
Georgia Chutney (recipe follows)

Preheat the oven to 350°F. Sprinkle the pork loins with the 4 teaspoons salt and roll them in the pepper to coat evenly. Place the pork loins in a metal baking pan and bake in the preheated oven, turning occasionally to form a crisp crust, until they reach an internal temperature of 135°F.

Meanwhile, place the beans in a steamer basket over boiling water, cover, and steam until crisp-tender, about 3 minutes. Rinse under cold water and drain. Season with salt and pepper.

Slice the pork tenderloin on the diagonal and divide the slices evenly among 4 plates, fanning them in the 6 o'clock position on the plate. Place a scoop of the buttermilk mashed potatoes at 9 o'clock. Place a large dollop of Georgia chutney in the center of each plate.

Makes 4 servings

Per Serving (without chutney or mashed potatoes)
Calories 240 • Carbohydrates 7 g • Cholesterol 100 mg
Fat 6 g • Protein 37 g • Sodium 2,215 mg

Carbo's Cafe

Georgia Chutney

2 peaches, peeled, halved, pitted, and diced
1½ teaspoons butter
1 Vidalia or other sweet white onion, diced
⅓ cup chopped pecans
¼ cup packed brown sugar
2 tablespoons granulated sugar
½ cup cider vinegar
¼ cup red wine vinegar
¼ cup dark corn syrup
¼ cup light corn syrup

Bring a medium saucepan of water to a simmer, gently drop in the peaches, and cook for 30 seconds. Using a slotted spoon, transfer the peaches to a bowl of ice water. When cool, slip the skins off the peaches, then pit and dice them.

In a large saucepan over medium heat, melt the butter and sauté the onion and pecans until the onion is translucent, about 5 minutes. Add the peaches and cook for 3 minutes. Stir in the remaining ingredients. Bring to a boil, reduce heat to low, and simmer the chutney, stirrring occasionally, for 45 minutes, or until the mixture is thickened and reduced by two thirds.

Makes about 1 cup

Per Serving
Calories 150 • Carbohydrates 31 g • Cholesterol 0 mg
Fat 4 g • Protein 1 g • Sodium 40 mg

Carbo's Cafe

Buttermilk Mashed Potatoes

1½ pounds Idaho potatoes, peeled and diced
2 tablespoons salt
2 tablespoons butter
1 to 2 cups warm buttermilk
1½ teaspoons salt
½ teaspoon ground white pepper

Place the potatoes in salted water to cover in a large pot; bring the water to a low boil. Cook for 10 to 15 minutes, or until the potatoes are tender. Drain and transfer the potatoes to a large bowl. Using a mixer with a whisk attachment or a hand-held potato masher, whip or mash the potatoes and mix in the butter, buttermilk, salt, and pepper until smooth. Serve immediately or cover and keep warm in a double boiler.

Makes 4 servings

Per Serving
Calories 220 • Carbohydrates 37 g • Cholesterol less than 5 mg
Fat 6 g • Protein 5 g • Sodium 1,340 mg

Genoise with Blackberry Compote and Yogurt Crème Fraîche

Genoise
½ cup packed brown sugar

4 eggs

¾ cup plus 2 tablespoons unbleached all-purpose flour, sifted

Yogurt Crème Fraîche
¼ cup plain low-fat yogurt

2 tablespoons buttermilk

Blackberry Compote
1 cup fresh orange juice

¼ cup granulated sugar

1 tablespoon arrowroot

1 tablespoon water

4 cups fresh blackberries

6 fresh mint sprigs for garnish

Sifted confectioners' sugar for garnish

To make the genoise: Preheat the oven to 375°F. Grease and flour a loaf pan. In a large bowl, beat the brown sugar and eggs at high speed until they are tripled in volume. Quickly mix the flour into the egg mixture. Immediately pour the mixture into the prepared pan. Bake in the preheated oven for 25 to 30 minutes, or until a toothpick inserted in the center of the cake comes out clean. Let cool in the pan on a wire rack for 10 minutes, then unmold onto the rack to cool completely.

To make the yogurt crème fraîche: In a medium bowl, stir together the yogurt and buttermilk; let stand at room temperature for 1 hour.

To make the blackberry compote: In a small saucepan over medium heat, stir together the orange juice and sugar and bring to a simmer. Dissolve

Carbo's Cafe

the arrowroot in the water. Add the arrowroot mixture and stir constantly until the mixture thickens. Gently stir in the blackberries and keep warm.

To serve, preheat the oven to 400°F. Cut 4 slices from the cake, place them on a baking sheet, and warm in the preheated oven for 5 minutes. Place a slice of cake in the center of each of 4 dessert plates and spoon some of the blackberry compote over. Top with yogurt crème frâiche and a mint sprig. Dust the edge of each plate with confectioners' sugar.

Makes one cake; serves 6

Per Serving
Calories 250 • Carbohydrates 58 g • Cholesterol less than 5 mg
Fat 1 g • Protein 6 g • Sodium 60 mg

Centro Grill and Wine Bar

Toronto, Ontario

Centro Grill and Wine Bar hums with energy and is one of Toronto's most popular dining spots. Partners Franco Prevedello, Tony Longo, and Marc Thuet have created a large trendsetting restaurant bright with skylights, high ceilings, mirrors, and powerful colors.

Chef Marc Thuet's seasonal menu blends classic and innovative Continental cuisine, with an emphasis on robust flavors. The comprehensive selection of international wines has received *The Wine Spectator's* Best of Award of Excellence. The following recipes were created by chef Marc Thuet.

Centro Grill and Wine Bar

THE MENU
Centro Grill and Wine Bar

⨎

Crisp Striped Bass and Lobster

Medallions of Veal Tenderloin with Leek and Wild Mushroom Ragôut

Délices des Alpes with Two Sauces and Green Tea Sorbet

Serves Four

Centro Grill and Wine Bar

Crisp Striped Bass and Lobster

Fish Mousse

2 ounces striped bass tails or sea bass scraps, skinned and boned

½ egg white

2 tablespoons non-fat quark or ricotta cheese

Freshly ground black pepper, salt, and fresh lemon juice to taste

Exotic Essence

1 tablespoon minced shallots

½ vanilla bean, halved lengthwise

⅓ cup apple juice

¼ cup pineapple juice

Salt, freshly ground black pepper, and lemon juice to taste

8 cups court bouillon (see page 226) or water

Two 1-pound live lobsters

3 ounces asparagus

¼ cup fresh or thawed frozen green peas

Four 3-ounce striped bass or sea bass fillets

Salt and freshly ground black pepper to taste

1 tablespoon olive oil

Minced fresh chives for garnish

12 fresh chervil sprigs and diced mango for garnish (optional)

To make the fish mousse: To a blender or food processor, add the bass scraps and purée. Add the egg white, cheese, salt, pepper, and lemon and blend until smooth. Adjust the seasoning. Cover and refrigerate.

To make the exotic essence: In a nonstick saucepan over low heat, sauté the shallots and vanilla bean for 3 minutes. Add the apple and pineapple juices and bring to a simmer. Remove from heat and strain through cheese-cloth. Season with salt, pepper, and lemon juice; set aside.

Bring the court bouillon or water to a boil over high heat. Kill the lobsters by making an incision in the back of the shell where the chest and tail meet. Plunge the lobsters into it, and cook for 1 minute. Remove the saucepan from heat and place in a large bowl of ice. Set aside to cool.

Blanch the asparagus in boiling salted water for 2 to 4 minutes, or until crisp-tender; drain and plunge into cold water. Cut the asparagus tips into 1-inch lengths. Cut the stems into small pieces. In a medium bowl, gently combine the asparagus and peas; set aside.

When the lobsters have cooled, remove the tails. Shell the tails by cutting through the underside of the shell with scissors. Remove the claws and carefully shell them, removing and discarding any cartilage. Cut the tails into medallions about ¼ inch thick and set them aside with the claw meat.

Season the bass fillets with salt and pepper. Using a spatula, spread one side of the fillets with a little of the fish mousse.

Preheat the oven to 350°F. In a nonstick frying pan over high heat, heat half of the olive oil and sear the fish fillets, mousse-side down, until golden brown. Carefully transfer the fillets to a baking pan, placing them mousse-side up. Bake in the preheated oven for 2 minutes, or until the fish is opaque throughout.

In another nonstick frying pan over high heat, heat the remaining half of the olive oil and sauté the lobster meat for 5 to 10 seconds, to heat through. Add the asparagus and peas and sauté for another 20 to 30 seconds to heat through.

Arrange one-fourth of the lobster meat and the asparagus-pea mixture in an attractive manner in the center of each of 4 plates. Top each with a bass fillet and spoon some of the exotic essence over. Garnish with the chives and optional chervil and mango and serve at once.

Makes 4 servings

Per Serving
Calories 350 • Carbohydrates 31 g • Cholesterol 120 mg
Fat 8 g • Protein 37 g • Sodium 600 mg

Centro Grill and Wine Bar

Medallions of Veal Tenderloin with Leek and Wild Mushroom Ragôut

If you can't find black chanterelles, use a total of 10 ounces of chanterelles.

Tarragon Sauce

1¼ cups brown chicken stock (see page 225)

1 tablespoon minced fresh tarragon

Salt and freshly ground black pepper to taste

2 leeks, white part only, cut into ⅜-inch crosswise pieces

12 baby carrots, with part of the green top on

8 baby turnips, with part of the green top on

8 patty pan (scallop) squash

4 baby zucchini

8 baby corn ears

1 pound veal tenderloins, cut into 8 pieces

Salt and freshly ground pepper to taste

1 tablespoon olive oil

1 tablespoon minced shallots

3 ounces oyster mushrooms

4 ounces chanterelles

6 ounces black chanterelles (black trumpet mushrooms)

Minced chives or chervil to taste

To make the tarragon sauce: In a saucepan over high heat, cook the brown chicken stock to reduce it by half or three quarters. Add the tarragon and season with salt and pepper. Set aside.

Blanch the leeks for 30 seconds in boiling salted water; drain and cool in ice water for 2 minutes. Blanch the baby carrots, turnips, squash, zucchini and corn for 1½ to 2 minutes; drain and cool in ice water. Slice the baby zucchini into fan shapes. Dry the vegetables on paper towels and set aside.

Season the veal medallions with salt and pepper. In a nonstick skillet or sauté pan over high heat, heat half the oil and sauté the veal for about 1 minute on each side. Remove from the pan and keep warm. In the same skillet or sauté pan, heat the remaining olive oil and sauté the shallots until translucent, about 3 minutes. Remove the shallots from the pan with a slotted spoon and set aside. Return the pan to high heat and sauté all of the mushrooms for about 1 minute. Add the leeks and stir constantly for another 1 to 2 minutes. Lower the heat to medium and add the other blanched vegetables. Add the shallots and season with salt and pepper to taste. Set aside and cover to keep warm.

Place equal amounts of the leek and wild mushroom ragôut in the center of each of 4 warmed plates. Top each serving of ragôut with 2 veal medallions. Arrange the vegetables in an attractive manner on each plate. Ladle the warm tarragon sauce over the veal and around the ragôut. Garnish each plate with chives or chervil; serve at once.

Makes 4 servings

Per Serving
Calories 390 • Carbohydrates 29 g • Cholesterol 115 mg
Fat 12 g • Protein 44 g • Sodium 240 mg

Centro Grill and Wine Bar

Délices des Alpes with Two Sauces and Green Tea Sorbet

Begin this recipe 3 hours before serving.

⅘ cup confectioners' sugar, sifted

6 tablespoons unbleached all-purpose flour

3 large egg whites

Pinch of salt

¼ cup slivered almonds

2 teaspoons grated orange zest

1 pound mixed fresh berries such as raspberries, blackberries,
  strawberries, or other seasonal fruits

Green Tea Sorbet

1⅔ cups water

2 tablespoons green tea

⅓ cup granulated sugar

1 tablespoon honey

Juice of 1 lime

2 egg whites

Raspberry Sauce

1¼ cup fresh or thawed frozen unsweetened raspberries

2 tablespoons confectioners' sugar, sifted

Juice of ½ lemon

Yogurt Sauce

⅓ cup non-fat plain yogurt

Juice of ½ lemon

2 tablespoons confectioners' sugar, sifted, for garnish

4 fresh mint sprigs for garnish

In a medium bowl, combine the confectioners' sugar, flour, egg whites, and salt to make a thick batter. Stir in the orange zest and almonds. Cover and let rest for 3 hours in the refrigerator.

Preheat the oven to 350°F. Using a small rubber spatula, spread the batter into four 8-inch diameter circles on nonstick or parchment-covered baking sheets. Bake in the preheated oven for 8 minutes, or until golden. Quickly remove a circle from the baking sheet and place it over an inverted cup so that it droops into a basket shape; repeat until all the circles are molded. Let cool.

To make the green tea sorbet: Bring the water to a boil, pour it over the green tea, and let steep for 2 to 3 minutes. Strain the tea into a medium bowl. Stir in the sugar and honey until dissolved. Add the lime juice and set aside to cool.

Transfer to an ice cream maker and partially freeze according to the manufacturer's directions. In a medium bowl, beat the egg whites until stiff peaks form. Carefully fold the egg whites into the partially frozen tea. Continue freezing until completely frozen.

To make the raspberry sauce: In a blender or food processor, purée the raspberries. Strain through a fine-meshed sieve into a medium saucepan over medium heat. Stir in the sugar and lemon juice and bring the mixture to a simmer. Remove from heat and let cool.

To make the yogurt sauce: In a small bowl, whisk together the yogurt and lemon juice.

Wash the berries and/or fruits and dry them on paper towels. Sprinkle the baskets with the confectioners' sugar and arrange the berries in them. Pour the raspberry and yogurt sauces in the center of each of 4 plates. Place a fruit basket in the center of each plate. Add 1 scoop of green tea sorbet to each basket. Garnish with a mint sprig and serve at once.

Makes 4 servings

Per Serving
Calories 440 • Carbohydrates 95 g • Cholesterol 0 mg
Fat 4.5 g • Protein 10 g • Sodium 110 mg

Centro Grill and Wine Bar

Chanterelles

Philadelphia, Pennsylvania

Chef Philippe Chin opened Chanterelles in 1992 and received immediate critical acclaim for his light, artfully presented dishes. Chin is a culinary artist whose cooking style blends classic French and contemporary techniques and ingredients. Trained at L'Ecole Hôtelière de Paris in France, he was named one of the top ten culinary students in the city by Les Maîtres Cuisiniers de France. After working at prestigious restaurants and hotels in France and the Caribbean, he was chef at The Rittenhouse in Philadelphia before launching Chanterelles. Explaining his cooking style, Chin says, "For me, my food is a lot of surprise, a lot of texture, and the most imporant thing is that all the food on the plate should work together." *Esquire* magazine selected Chin as a Rising Star Chef in 1993.

Chanterelles offers seasonal à la carte specialties as well as tasting, vegetarian, and pre-theater menus that emphasize a playful approach resulting from chef Chin's constant experimenting. Chin says he became a chef "because I love to play with food!" Cooking is fun, says Chin. "It depends on my mood, and no matter what my mood is, I never try to have the same fun twice." Chanterelle's wine list of French and American vintages has won *The Wine Spectator's* Award of Excellence.

THE MENU
Chanterelles

Wild Mushroom Consommé

Coho Salmon Salad with Corn Coulis

Venison Cutlets En Habit Vert

Individual Nectarine Tartes Tatin

Serves Two

Wild Mushroom Consommé

1 ounce dried porcini mushrooms

1 cup hot water

2 cups chicken stock (see page 225) or canned low-salt chicken broth

3 ounces fresh shiitake mushrooms, stemmed and
    cut into ⅛-inch-thick strips

3 ounces fresh oyster mushrooms, stemmed and sliced

3 ounces fresh chanterelle or other seasonal mushrooms,
    stemmed and sliced

Salt and freshly ground black pepper to taste

Minced fresh parsley for garnish

Place the dried mushrooms in a small bowl, add the hot water, and set aside for 2 hours. Drain the dried mushrooms, reserving the soaking liquid.

In a large saucepan, bring the stock or broth to a simmer. Add the soaked dried mushrooms and simmer for 30 minutes.

Using a slotted spoon, remove the dried mushrooms from the stock or broth; discard or save them for another use. Add all but the last ½ inch of the mushroom soaking liquid and the fresh mushrooms to the broth; simmer for 10 minutes. Season the soup with salt and pepper, sprinkle with parsley, and serve.

Makes 2 servings

Per Serving
Calories 110 • Carbohydrates 21 g • Cholesterol 0 mg
Fat 1.5 g • Protein 6 g • Sodium 50 mg

Chanterelles

Coho Salmon Salad with Corn Coulis

Corn Coulis

1 ear fresh corn

2 tablespoons chicken stock (see page 225) or
   canned low-salt chicken broth

1 tablespoon extra-virgin olive oil

Salt and freshly ground black pepper to taste

Two 4-ounce coho salmon fillets

Salt and freshly ground black pepper to taste

2 tablespoons mild olive oil

2 tablespoons peanut oil

2 handfuls mixed baby greens

Herb Vinaigrette (recipe follows)

To make the corn coulis: Shuck the corn and, using a sharp knife, cut the kernels from the cob. In a medium saucepan, bring the stock or broth to a boil. Add the corn kernels and boil for 10 minutes. Remove from heat and pour the broth and corn into a blender or food processor; blend until smooth. Blend in the olive oil, salt, and pepper. Pour the corn coulis back in the saucepan; set aside and keep warm.

Dry the salmon fillets with paper towels and season with salt and pepper. In a large skillet or sauté pan over medium heat, heat the olive and peanut oils and sauté the fillets until golden brown, about 3 minutes on each side. Place the salmon in the center of each of 4 plates and surround with the warm corn coulis. Toss the lettuces with some of the herb vinaigrette and top each fillet with some salad.

Makes 2 servings

Per Serving (without Herb Vinaigrette)
Calories 330 • Carbohydrates 10 g • Cholesterol 55 mg
Fat 21 g • Protein 25 g • Sodium 80 mg

Chanterelles

Herb Vinaigrette

¼ teaspoon Dijon mustard

½ tablespoon balsamic vinegar

Salt and freshly ground black pepper to taste

¼ cup extra-virgin olive oil

½ teaspoon minced fresh tarragon

½ teaspoon minced fresh chervil

½ teaspoon minced fresh basil

½ teaspoon minced fresh parsley

In a small bowl, whisk together the mustard, vinegar, salt, and pepper. Whisk in the olive oil in a steady stream. Stir in the remaining ingredients.

Makes about ¼ cup

Per Serving
Calories 130 • Carbohydrates 0 g • Cholesterol 0 mg
Fat 14 g • Protein 0 g • Sodium 10 mg

Venison Cutlets En Habit Vert

Rich and full of flavor, venison is also low in fat and cholesterol. Here, it is dressed in a coating of minced fresh herbs and served with an Asian-flavored sauce.

½ tablespoon each minced fresh basil, chervil, mint, cilantro,
    and flat-leaf (Italian) parsley
½ tablespoon olive oil
Four 3-ounce venison cutlets
½ tablespoon olive oil
½ tablespoon Asian sesame oil
½ tablespoon minced garlic
½ tablespoon low-salt soy sauce
½ tablespoon minced shallots
½ tablespoon freshly grated unpeeled fresh ginger
⅓ cup chicken stock (see page 225) or canned low-salt chicken broth
1 teaspoon butter

Preheat the oven to 400°F. In a small bowl, mix together the minced herbs; set aside.

In a large skillet or sauté pan over medium-high heat, heat the olive oil and sear the venison cutlets for 2 minutes on each side. Transfer the cutlets to a baking pan and coat each cutlet on both sides with the sesame oil and mixed herbs.

Add the garlic, soy sauce, shallots, ginger, and stock or broth to the skillet or sauté pan and cook over medium heat for about 3 minutes. Whisk in the butter until melted.

Heat the venison in the preheated oven for about 2 minutes. Divide the venison cutlets among 2 plates, ladle the sauce over, and serve immediately.

Makes 2 servings

Per Serving
Calories 390 • Carbohydrates 2 g • Cholesterol 140 mg
Fat 24 g • Protein 38 g • Sodium 620 mg

Individual Nectarine Tartes Tatin

¼ cup sugar
2 tablespoons unsalted butter
1 tablespoon water
1 large nectarine, halved lengthwise and pitted
3 ounces thawed frozen puff pastry
Vanilla ice cream or frozen yogurt for serving (optional)

Preheat the oven to 375°F. In a heavy, medium saucepan over medium heat, stir the sugar and butter together until the mixture is golden brown, watching carefully to keep it from burning. Whisk in the water and immediately remove the caramel from heat. Pour equal amounts of the caramel to coat the bottom of two 4½-inch tartlet molds.

With the cut side down, thinly slice the nectarines. Fan half the nectarine slices over the caramel in each tartlet mold.

Roll out the puff pastry on a lightly floured board to a ⅛-inch thickness and cut two 4-inch-diameter circles. Cover the nectarines with the puff pastry circles. Bake the tartlets in the preheated oven for 15 minutes, or until the pastry is golden brown.

Let cool slightly on a wire rack. Reverse the tarts onto 2 serving plates to unmold. Serve with vanilla ice cream or frozen yogurt, if desired.

Makes 2 servings

Per Serving (without ice cream or frozen yogurt)
Calories 470 • Carbohydrates 52 g • Cholesterol 30 mg
Fat 28 g • Protein 4 g • Sodium 110 mg

Chef Allen's Restaurant

Aventura, Florida

Chef Allen's is headquarters for distinguished chef Allen Susser. After developing his classical cooking technique in the kitchens of Le Bristol Hotel in Paris and Le Cirque Restaurant in New York, in 1986, Susser opened Chef Allen's in Aventura, about a half-hour's drive north of downtown Miami. There he has adapted his contemporary cooking techniques to South Florida's tropical ingredients and developed the innovative culinary style he calls New World cuisine. Susser's inspiration has now expanded beyond his local region, and he incorporates Caribbean, Latin American, and modern American influences in his cooking. Some of his favorite ingredients are mango, starfruit, mamey, cobia, wahoo, pompano, Scotch bonnet, vanilla, and rum.

Chef Allen's Art Deco dining room is highlighted by an exhibition kitchen, glass block wall, neon trim, and fresh flowers. Allen Susser received the James Beard Foundation's Best Chef Award Southeast region, in 1994, and *Food and Wine* magazine named him Best New Chef in America in 1991. Susser explains his philosophy: "I love to cook, and so food is my life, my profession, my charity, and my diversion." He travels frequently to the Caribbean and Latin America, where he donates his talents to local charity and organizes exchanges on food and preparation with Caribbean and Latin chefs.

THE MENU
Chef Allen's

✧

Curried Lobster with Plaintains

Yuca Mojo with Green Olives and Orange Salad

Roast Free-Range Jerked Chicken

Caribbean Ratatouille

Pain Perdu with Mango and Chocolate Sorbets

Serves Four

Chef Allen's Restaurant

Curried Lobster with Plaintains

Plantains are vegetable-like bananas with a bland flavor that are eaten ripe and unripe, but never raw. The skin of plantains is black when they are fully ripened.

2 tablespoons olive oil
3 large shallots, diced
1½ pounds cooked lobster meat, cut into 1-inch pieces
1 teaspoon minced garlic
½ teaspoon minced fresh ginger
3 tablespoons curry powder
1 tablespoon ground turmeric
2 cups coconut milk
1 teaspoon coarse sea salt
½ teaspoon freshly ground black pepper
1 large ripe plantain, peeled and cut into 1-inch pieces
2 tablespoons finely chopped green onion
Fresh lime juice to taste

In a heavy pot over medium heat, heat the olive oil and sauté the shallots until translucent, about 3 minutes. Add the lobster meat and sauté for 1 minute. Stir in the garlic, ginger, curry powder, turmeric, and coconut milk and bring to a simmer. Season with salt and pepper, add the plantain, and simmer for 5 more minutes. Divide the curried lobster among 4 shallow bowls, sprinkle with the green onion and lime juice, and serve.

Makes 4 servings

Per Serving
Calories 600 • Carbohydrates 33 g • Cholesterol 120 mg
Fat 37 g • Protein 39 g • Sodium 1,250 mg

Chef Allen's Restaurant

Yuca Mojo with Green Olives and Orange Salad

The cassava, called yuca in Spanish, is a white-fleshed tuber with a brown skin. Believed native to South America, it is also known as manioc.

1 pound cassava, peeled and cut into 3-inch pieces
   (Available in Latino markets)
1 tablespoon coarse sea salt

Mojo
1 tablespoon olive oil
1 large onion, diced
1 tablespoon minced garlic
1 cup fresh orange juice
3 tablespoons fresh lime juice
2 tablespoons minced fresh cilantro

Orange Salad
2 navel oranges, peeled and cut into sections (see page 232)
1 small red onion, finely chopped
1 teaspoon salt
1 teaspoon pink peppercorns
1 teaspoon rum

½ cup chopped pitted green olives
1 tablespoon minced fresh cilantro for garnish

In a medium saucepan, bring the cassava, water to cover, and salt to a boil, reduce the heat to low, and simmer for 45 minutes, or until the cassava is tender. Remove from heat and let the cassava sit in its cooking liquid until cool. Using a slotted spoon, remove the cassava pieces and cut them into quarters.

To prepare the mojo: In a medium saucepan over medium heat, combine the olive oil, onion, garlic, orange juice, and lime juice and simmer for

Chef Allen's Restaurant

10 minutes. Remove from heat and stir in the cilantro.

To prepare the orange salad: In a medium bowl, combine all the ingredients. Cover with plastic wrap and refrigerate for 1 hour.

To serve, return the mojo to high heat, carefully stir in the cassava pieces, and cook for 1 minute. Remove from heat and stir in the olives. Divide the mojo among 4 serving bowls, top with orange salad, and sprinkle with the cilantro.

Makes 4 servings

Per Serving
Calories 280 • Carbohydrates 53 g • Cholesterol 0 mg
Fat 6 g • Protein 6 g • Sodium 1,020 mg

Chef Allen's Restaurant

Roast Free-Range Jerked Chicken

Jerk Seasoning

¼ cup ground allspice

1 teaspoon ground cinnamon

½ teaspoon ground nutmeg

1 tablespoon minced fresh cilantro

4 green onions with tops, chopped

2 tablespoons minced garlic

1 teaspoon tamarind (available in Latino markets)

1 cup dry red wine

¼ cup olive oil

1 teaspoon coarse sea salt

1 teaspoon minced Scotch Bonnet (habañero) chili

One 3-pound free-range chicken

In a medium bowl, stir together all the jerk seasoning ingredients. Cover the bowl with plastic wrap and set aside at room temperature for 30 minutes.

Preheat the oven to 350°F. Wearing rubber gloves, coat the chicken inside and out with the jerk seasoning, place it in a baking pan, and let it sit for 15 minutes. Place the chicken on the middle shelf of the preheated oven and bake for 45 minutes. Lower the heat to 325°F and bake for another 20 minutes, or until the juices run clear when the thighs are pierced. Let the chicken sit for 5 minutes before slicing.

Makes 4 servings

Per Serving
Calories 450 • Carbohydrates 5 g • Cholesterol 130 mg
Fat 27 g • Protein 42 g • Sodium 420 mg

Chef Allen's Restaurant

Caribbean Ratatouille

3 tablespoons olive oil
1 large onion, diced
1 small eggplant, diced
1 small green plantain, peeled and diced
2 chayotes,* diced
2 Anaheim chilies,** seeded and diced
1 red bell pepper, cored, seeded, and diced
2 large tomatoes, peeled, seeded, and diced
½ tablespoon minced garlic
1 tablespoon fresh oregano
1 tablespoon ground cumin
1 teaspoon freshly ground black pepper
½ cup dry white wine
2 teaspoons salt

In a large Dutch oven or heavy pot over medium heat, heat the olive oil and sauté the onion until translucent, about 5 minutes. Stir in the eggplant and cook for 1 minute. Carefully stir in each vegetable, one at a time, at 1-minute intervals; try to not crush any of the vegetables.

Stir in the remaining ingredients and simmer for 5 minutes. Serve at once or set aside and serve at room temperature.

Makes 4 to 6 servings

* The chayote, also called a mirleton, is a pear-shaped winter squash with a thin, light green skin, one large seed, and a delicate taste. It is available in some supermarkets and in Latino markets.
** Anaheim chilies are elongated red or green, cone-shaped peppers with a slight twist toward the end.

Per Serving
Calories 180 • Carbohydrates 27 g • Cholesterol 0 mg
Fat 8 g • Protein 3 g • Sodium 730 mg

Chef Allen's Restaurant

Pain Perdu with Mango and Chocolate Sorbets

½ cup milk

1 large egg

2 tablespoons vanilla extract

¼ teaspoon ground ginger

¼ teaspoon ground cinnamon

Pinch of salt

½ loaf brioche, cut into ¾-inch-thick slices

1 tablespoon butter

1 cup mango sorbet

1 cup chocolate sorbet

In a medium bowl, lightly beat together the milk, egg, vanilla, ginger, cinnamon, and salt. Dip the slices of brioche in this mixture and allow to soak for 30 seconds.

In a large sauté pan or skillet over medium heat, melt a little of the butter, add a few slices of the soaked brioche, and cook on both sides until slightly crisp and golden in color. Place in a warm oven and repeat to cook the remaining slices in batches. Divide slices of pain perdu among 4 plates and top with a scoop of mango and chocolate sorbet. Serve at once.

Makes 4 servings

Per Serving
Calories 310 • Carbohydrates 46 g • Cholesterol 95 mg
Fat 9 g • Protein 9 g • Sodium 420 mg

The Classic Kitchen

Noblesville, Indiana

The Classic Kitchen is the realized dream of chef and marathon runner Steve Keneipp. After receiving a master's degree in nutrition, he wanted to create a restaurant in his native Indiana that would "feed all of the senses, not just the palate." In 1980, he opened The Classic Kitchen in Noblesville, about twenty miles northwest of Indianapolis.

The innovative and carefully balanced menu makes the most of natural ingredients. Keneipp creates sumptuous yet healthful dishes by reducing fat content without reducing flavor. Diners enjoy recorded performances of chamber music in the Classic Kitchen's charming forty-seat dining room. Keneipp is a community nutritionist for St. Vincent's Hospital and an active member of the Institute of American Culinary Professionals. His talent as a food consultant is now sought by restaurateurs around the world.

THE MENU
The Classic Kitchen

Polenta with Goat Cheese and Sun-dried Tomatoes

White Bean and Almond Soup

Breast of Chicken Dijonaise

Baby Carrots with Warm Raspberry Butter

Blueberry Pouches

Serves Four

The Classic Kitchen

Polenta with Goat Cheese and Sun-dried Tomatoes

1¼ cups water
¼ teaspoon salt
½ teaspoon dried oregano
¼ teaspoon freshly ground black pepper
¾ cup polenta (coarsely ground cornmeal)
2 to 3 ounces fresh white goat cheese
16 black olive slices
2 tablespoons finely chopped sun-dried tomatoes
Minced fresh parsley or basil for garnish

In a large, heavy saucepan, combine the water, salt, oregano, and pepper and bring to a boil. Whisk in the polenta, lower the heat to medium, and cook for about 20 minutes, stirring constantly with a wooden spoon until the mixture has thickened.

Spray an 8-inch square pan with olive-oil cooking spray. Spread the polenta in the prepared pan, cover, and chill in the refrigerator until firm.

Preheat the oven to 425°F. Cut the polenta into 8 squares. Transfer the squares to a flat work surface and cut each in half diagonally. Top each triangle with a scant ½ teaspoon of goat cheese, 1 olive slice, and a sprinkle of dried tomatoes. Spray a baking sheet with olive-oil cooking spray. Place the polenta triangles on the prepared baking sheet and bake in the preheated oven for 10 to 12 minutes, or until the tomatoes begin to char. Sprinkle with parsley or basil and serve.

Makes 16 triangles; serves 4 as an appetizer

Per Serving
Calories 20 • Carbohydrates 2 g • Cholesterol less than 5 mg
Fat 1 g • Protein 1 g • Sodium 65 mg

The Classic Kitchen

White Bean and Almond Soup

1½ cups dried navy beans
1 onion, finely diced
1 garlic clove, minced
6 cups chicken stock (see page 225) or canned low-salt chicken broth
1 cup (4 ounces) blanched almonds, ground
½ cup dry white wine
Salt to taste
⅛ teaspoon ground white pepper
Minced fresh rosemary and whole lavender blossoms for garnish (optional)
Sliced almonds, toasted (see page 232), for garnish (optional)

Rinse and pick through the beans, place them in a bowl, cover with cold water, and soak overnight; drain.

In a large, heavy pot over high heat, bring the beans, onion, garlic, and stock or broth to a boil. Reduce the heat to low and simmer, stirring frequently, until the beans are tender, about 1 hour. Stir in the ground almonds and wine.

Transfer the mixture to a blender or food processor and purée, in batches if necesary, adding more broth if necessary. Season with salt and pepper. Ladle into 4 soup bowls and garnish with rosemary and lavender blossoms and sliced almonds, if desired.

Makes 4 servings

Per Serving (without rosemary, lavender blossoms, or almond garnishes)
Calories 480 • Carbohydrates 56 g • Cholesterol 75 mg
Fat 17 g • Protein 27 g • Sodium 75 mg

The Classic Kitchen

Breast of Chicken Dijonaise

Mustard Sauce

I cup Dijon mustard
¾ cup dry white wine, chicken stock (see page 225),
   or canned low-salt chicken broth
2 teaspoons minced fresh tarragon

4 chicken breast halves, boned, skinned, and flattened with a mallet
Dry white wine, chicken stock (see page 225), or canned low-salt
   chicken broth to cover
2 tablespoons olive oil
4 fresh lemon slices

To make the sauce: In a small bowl, whisk together the mustard, wine, stock, or broth, and tarragon. Cover and set aside.

Preheat the oven to 325°F. Lightly coat a baking dish with olive oil and add the chicken breasts. Add the wine, stock, or broth to just cover the chicken and top with the olive oil. Cover the dish with aluminum foil and bake in the preheated oven for 30 minutes, or until opaque throughout with just a hint of pinkness. Cover and refrigerate if making ahead.

Preheat the oven to 425°F. Place half of the mustard sauce and the lemon slices in the bottom of a baking dish just large enough to hold the chicken. Add the poached chicken breasts and coat them with the remaining sauce. Cover the pan with aluminum foil and bake in the preheated oven for about 10 minutes, or 20 minutes if the chicken was chilled. Serve topped with some of the sauce.

Makes 4 servings

Per Serving
Calories 280 • Carbohydrates 7 g • Cholesterol 75 mg
Fat 14 g • Protein 30 g • Sodium 1,200 mg

The Classic Kitchen

Baby Carrots with Warm Raspberry Butter

Raspberry Butter
3 tablespoons raspberry vinegar
1 tablespoon unsalted butter
Freshly ground black pepper to taste

8 ounces baby carrots, quartered lengthwise

To make the raspberry butter: In a small saucepan over medium heat, combine all the ingredients and cook until the butter melts. Set aside and keep warm.

Fill a medium saucepan with water, bring to a boil, and cook the carrots until crisp-tender, about 5 minutes; drain. Serve the carrots drizzled with warm raspberry butter.

Makes 4 servings

Per Serving
Calories 50 • Carbohydrates 7 g • Cholesterol 10 mg
Fat 3 g • Protein less than 1 g • Sodium 20 mg

Blueberry Pouches

¾ cup unthawed frozen blueberries
¾ tablespoon unbleached all-purpose flour
Pinch of ground cloves
¾ tablespoon orange marmalade, melted
4 sheets thawed frozen phyllo dough
Butter-flavored cooking spray for coating
Sifted confectioners' sugar for dusting
Sliced fresh strawberries and fresh mint sprigs for garnish

Preheat the oven to 400°F and line a sided baking sheet with aluminum foil or parchment paper. In a large bowl, combine the blueberries, flour, cloves, and melted marmalade.

Lay 1 phyllo sheet on a work surface and spray it lightly with butter-flavored cooking spray. (Cover the remaining phyllo with plastic wrap and a damp cloth.) Cut the sprayed phyllo into quarters and gently stack the 4 sections on top of each other. Place the stack on a damp cloth and cover with a second damp cloth. Repeat to make 4 stacks. Place 2 tablespoons of the blueberry filling in the center of each stack and gently gather up the edges, pinching them together to close the phyllo into a little pouch.

Place the pouches on the prepared baking sheet and bake for 20 minutes, or until golden brown. Dust the pouches with a little confectioners' sugar and serve warm, garnished with a few sliced strawberries and a mint sprig or two.

Makes 4 servings

Per Serving (without sugar, strawberry, or mint garnishes)
Calories 110 • Carbohydrates 23 g • Cholesterol 0 mg
Fat 2 g • Protein less than 1.5 g • Sodium 95 mg

The Classic Kitchen

Ernie's

San Francisco, California

Ernie's Restaurant has achieved international recognition for the uncompromising quality of its cuisine, wine, and service thanks to the dedication of proprietors Victor and Roland Gotti. Their legendary restaurant has been awarded the coveted Five-Star Award from the Mobil Travel Guide for thirty years, longer than any other restaurant in the United States.

Opened in 1907, Ernie's was acquired in 1934 by Ernie Carlesso and his partner Ambrogio Gotti, Roland and Victor's father. Remaining a family affair ever since, the restaurant is now under the assured guidance of Victor's son-in-law Terence Fischer. The restaurant is housed in a classic brick building that was constructed following the 1906 San Francisco earthquake. Ernie's elaborate bar, with its fluted columns and Tiffany stained glass, was the setting for a famous scene in Alfred Hitchcock's movie Vertigo.

The menu features contemporary French cuisine that highlights complex flavors and simple, elegant presentation. Diners may choose from the chef's dégustation menu, a prix-fixe menu, or daily-changing à la carte selections. Two beautiful dining rooms are decorated with champagne-colored silk wall coverings, flowers, paintings, tapestried upholstery, and Victorian woodwork. Private dining rooms include the upstairs Ambrosia Room, with its elegant Victorian ambience, and the Bacchus Cellar, an unforgettable setting built into a portion of Ernie's renowned wine cellar. The following menu and recipes were created by executive chef David Kinch.

THE MENU

Ernie's

Acorn Squash Soup

Grilled Tuna with Vegetable Mignonette

Cranberry Soup with Fresh Fruit

Serves Two

Acorn Squash Soup

This recipe may be made 2 days before serving and reheated.

2 acorn squash
3 cups chicken stock (see page 225) or canned low-salt chicken broth
½ potato, peeled and sliced
1 small onion, sliced
3½ tablespoons maple syrup
2 teaspoons fresh lemon juice
Salt and white pepper to taste
2 tablespoons pecans, toasted (see page 232) and chopped

Preheat the oven to 400°F. Cut the acorn squash in half, remove the seeds and strings, and place the squash, cut-side down, on an oiled baking sheet. Bake in the preheated oven for 30 minutes, or until tender. Remove from the oven and let cool; peel and cube.

In a saucepan over medium heat, combine the acorn squash and stock or broth and bring to a simmer. Cook until the squash is heated through, about 5 minutes.

In a small saucepan over medium heat, simmer the potato and onion in salted water to cover until the potato is tender, about 15 minutes; drain. Add the potato and onion to the squash mixture.

Transfer the squash mixture to a blender or food processor and purée. Strain through a fine-meshed sieve into the saucepan. Stir in the maple syrup and lemon juice and season to taste with salt and pepper. Ladle into soup bowls and garnish with toasted pecans.

Makes 4 servings

Per Serving
Calories 190 • Carbohydrates 39 g • Cholesterol 0 mg
Fat 3.5 g • Protein less than 4 g • Sodium 40 mg

Grilled Tuna with Vegetable Mignonette

Vegetable Mignonette
1 small red bell pepper, roasted, peeled,
   and seeded (see page 232), finely diced
2 ounces baby green beans
½ small onion, finely diced
½ tablespoon capers, drained
1 teaspoon minced fresh parsley
Leaves from fresh thyme sprig, chopped coarsely
Pinch of freshly ground black pepper
⅓ cup fresh lemon juice
1 to 2 tablespoons olive oil (optional)
Salt to taste

Two 4-ounce ahi (yellowfin) tuna steaks at room temperature
2 teaspoons olive oil for brushing tuna
Salt and freshly ground black pepper to taste

To make the mignonette: In a large pot of boiling salted water, blanch the green beans for 2 or 3 minutes. Drain and immediately plunge the beans into a bowl of ice water. Drain and finely chop the beans.

In a large glass or ceramic bowl, stir together the onion, peppers, green beans, capers, parsley, thyme, pepper, lemon juice, and optional olive oil. Season with salt and let the vegetable mignonette marinate at room temperature for 2 hours, stirring occasionally.

Light a fire in a charcoal grill. Heat the cooking rack over very hot coals and oil it. Brush the tuna steaks with a little olive oil and season with salt and pepper. Grill the tuna until medium rare, about 3 to 4 minutes on each side.

Spoon the vegetable mignonette onto 2 warm plates and place the tuna steaks on top. The juices of the fish will intermingle with the marinade to form a natural vinaigrette. Serve immediately.

Makes 2 servings

Per Serving
Calories 200 • Carbohydrates 10 g • Cholesterol 50 mg
Fat 6 g • Protein 28 g • Sodium 105 mg

Cranberry Soup with Fresh Fruit

2 cups (8 ounces) fresh or frozen cranberries
⅓ cup honey
1 cup water
¼ cup dry white wine
Grated zest of ¼ lemon, ¼ lime, and ¼ orange
1 whole clove
¼ cinnamon stick
Assorted ripe seasonal fruits, cut into bite-sized pieces
Fresh mint leaves for garnish

In a nonaluminum saucepan over medium heat, bring the cranberries, honey, and water to a simmer and cook until most of the cranberries have burst, about 10 minutes.

Meanwhile, in a small saucepan, cook the wine, citrus zests, clove, and cinnamon over medium heat until the liquid is reduced by half.

Strain the cranberry liquid through a colander into another bowl and let drain completely without pressing the berries. This will prevent the liquid from becoming cloudy. Reserve the cranberries for another use.

Strain the spiced wine mixture through a fine-meshed sieve directly into the cranberry broth. Stir together the two liquids until well blended. Set the cranberry soup aside to cool.

Ladle the cranberry soup into shallow bowls and garnish with the seasonal fruits and fresh mint leaves.

Makes 2 servings

Per Serving (without fresh fruit or mint garnish)
Calories 230 • Carbohydrates 61 g • Cholesterol 0 mg
Fat 0 g • Protein 1 g • Sodium 10 mg

The Four Seasons Hotel
Chartwell Restaurant

Vancouver, British Columbia

Situated in the heart of the vibrant city of Vancouver, this grand hotel offers calm comfort, spacious luxury, and immediate access to cosmopolitan excitement. Its international acclaim includes the Five-Diamond Award from the American Automobile Association for nineteen consecutive years, and the coveted Mobil Travel Guide Four-Star Award for nineteen consecutive years.

Chartwell, the hotel's intimate fine-dining restaurant, is named after the summer home of Sir Winston Churchill. A large painting of the original Chartwell hangs prominently above the dining room fireplace. Paintings of the English countryside, classic wood paneling, parquet floors, and fresh flowers complete the dining room's country-manor ambience.

The menu of inventive Continental cuisine offers seasonal delicacies and Four Seasons Alternative Cuisine. Featuring health-conscious selections for gourmet tastes, Alternative Cuisine is lower in calories, cholesterol, sodium, and fat content. The wine list, featuring local estate wines, dessert wines, and vintage ports, has received *The Wine Spectator's* Best of Award of Excellence. The following menu and recipes were created by executive chef Marc Miron.

THE MENU
Chartwell Restaurant

ℐ

Chartwell Fresh Tomato Soup

Grilled Breast of Chicken on Hearts of Romaine with Mixed-Fruit Chutney

Angel Food Cake with Fresh Blackberry Coulis

Serves Four

Chartwell Restaurant

Chartwell Fresh Tomato Soup

½ tablespoon olive oil

½ onion, chopped

1 garlic clove, minced

4 beefsteak tomatoes, peeled, seeded, and chopped (see page 231)

½ cup tomato juice

½ tablespoon tomato paste

1½ cups chicken stock (see page 225) or canned low-salt chicken broth

¼ cup chopped fresh basil

1 bay leaf

½ tablespoon Worcestershire sauce

Salt and freshly ground black pepper to taste

4 basil sprigs for garnish

In a large saucepan over medium heat, heat the olive oil and sauté the onion and garlic until translucent, about 5 minutes. Add all the remaining ingredients except the basil sprigs and simmer gently for 30 minutes. Adjust the seasoning if necessary. Ladle the soup into 4 bowls and garnish with the basil sprigs.

Makes 4 servings

Per Serving
Calories 120 • Carbohydrates 23 g • Cholesterol 0 mg
Fat 3 g • Protein 5 g • Sodium 180 mg

Grilled Breast of Chicken on Hearts of Romaine with Mixed-Fruit Chutney

⅓ cup extra-virgin olive oil
4 teaspoons minced mixed fresh basil, cilantro, and parsley
Salt and cracked black pepper to taste
4 boneless chicken breast halves
2 romaine lettuce hearts, cut into quarters
¼ cup Herb Vinaigrette (see page 57)
Mixed-Fruit Chutney (recipe follows)

In a large bowl, combine the olive oil, herbs, salt, and pepper. Add the chicken, turn it to coat well, and let sit at room temperature for 1 hour. Heat a well-seasoned large cast-iron or nonstick pan over medium heat until very hot. Sear the chicken breasts, skin-side down, until golden, then turn and cook on the second side for about 7 minutes, or until golden on the second side and opaque throughout. Set aside.

To serve, arrange 2 quarters of romaine lettuce hearts on each of 4 plates and drizzle 1 tablespoon of the herb vinaigrette over. Slice the chicken, arrange the slices on top of the lettuce hearts, and garnish with the mixed-fruit chutney.

Makes 4 servings

Per Serving (without mixed-fruit chutney)
Calories 260 • Carbohydrates 3 g • Cholesterol 40 mg
Fat 20 g • Protein 15 g • Sodium 150 mg

Chartwell Restaurant

Mixed-Fruit Chutney

1 large pear, peeled, cored, and diced
1 large apple, peeled, cored, and diced
1 large peach, peeled, pitted, and diced
⅔ cup raisins
2 cups cider vinegar
½ teaspoon ground ginger
½ teaspoon ground mace
½ teaspoon ground allspice
1 bunch green onions, white parts only, finely chopped
Salt to taste

In a medium saucepan over low heat, cook all the ingredients for about 45 minutes to 1 hour, or until thickened. Cover and store any leftover chutney in the refrigerator for 1 week.

Makes about 2 cups

Per Serving
Calories 50 • Carbohydrates 14 g • Cholesterol 0 mg
Fat 0 g • Protein less than 1 g • Sodium 0 mg

Chartwell Restaurant

Angel Food Cake with Fresh Blackberry Coulis

Fresh Blackberry Coulis

4 cups fresh blackberries

¼ cup sugar

Juice of ½ lemon

Angel Food Cake

1¾ cups cake flour, sifted

2 cups sugar

16 egg whites

2 tablespoons vanilla extract

1 teaspoon cream of tartar

1 teaspoon salt

To make the blackberry coulis: Place the blackberries and sugar in a blender or food processor and blend until smooth. Stir in the lemon juice, strain through a fine-meshed sieve, and set aside.

To make the cake: Preheat the oven to 375°F. In a medium bowl, stir together the flour and 1½ cups of the sugar; set aside.

In a very large bowl, beat the egg whites and vanilla until soft peaks form. Gradually sprinkle in the cream of tartar, salt, and the remaining ½ cup sugar while beating until stiff but glossy peaks are formed. Gently fold in the flour-sugar mixture. Pour the batter into an ungreased 10-inch tube pan, cutting vertically through the batter several times with a rubber spatula to pop any air bubbles. Smooth the top with the rubber spatula.

Bake the cake in the preheated oven for about 30 minutes, or until the cake is spongy and a thin wooden skewer inserted in the center of the cake comes out clean. Invert the pan and let the cake cool completely. Remove the cake from the mold. Serve with the blackberry coulis.

Makes one 10-inch tube cake; serves 16

Per Serving
Calories 190 • Carbohydrates 42 g • Cholesterol 0 mg
Fat 0 g • Protein less than 5 g • Sodium 190 mg

Le Chardonnay

Los Angeles, California

Le Chardonnay is the inspiration of Robert Bigonnet and chef Claude Alrivy, two of the pioneers who helped make Los Angeles an innovative restaurant city. Alrivy and Bigonnet left the celebrated Le St. Germain to launch Le Chardonnay in 1984 and created a romantic French bistro tuned to Los Angeles tastes. Their restaurant is modeled after the interior of Vagenende, a century-old Parisian bistro with a considerable Art Nouveau collection that Bigonnet enjoyed during his law student days. Le Chardonnay's Belle Epoque interior includes arched mirrors, elaborate woodwork, hand-painted tiles, brass fixtures, and a wood-fired rotisserie.

Chef Alrivy's artfully prepared menu features traditional and California-style bistro food. For lovers of Chardonnay, the wine list has more than forty-five selections. Le Chardonnay provides a charming setting for a convivial crowd, and is one of the most popular restaurants in Los Angeles.

Le Chardonnay

THE MENU
Le Chardonnay

Baby Asparagus Vinaigrette with Crayfish

Mustard-Pepper Chicken with Herb Sauce

Apple Fritters

Serves Two

Baby Asparagus Vinaigrette with Crayfish

Crayfish are freshwater shellfish that look like tiny lobsters. There are two types available in North America, one from Louisiana and one from the West Coast.

1 pound baby asparagus
1 pound raw crayfish or jumbo shrimp
1 teaspoon fresh lemon juice
1 teaspoon red wine vinegar
2 teaspoons peanut oil
2 teaspoons olive oil
Salt and freshly ground black pepper to taste
5 fresh basil leaves, cut into fine shreds

Snap off the ends of the asparagus spears, wash, and drain. Cook the asparagus in boiling salted water for 2 or 3 minutes, or until the spears can be pierced with a fork but are still crunchy. Drain and immediately plunge the asparagus into cold water to set the bright green color; set aside.

In a large pot of boiling water, cook the crayfish or shrimp for 2 minutes. Using a slotted spoon, remove the crayfish or shrimp and let cool. Peel the tails only.

In a small bowl, whisk together the lemon juice, red wine vinegar, peanut oil, olive oil, salt, and pepper to make a vinaigrette.

Place the asparagus spears in the center of each of 2 plates and surround with the crayfish or prawns. Spoon the vinaigrette over and garnish with the basil.

Makes 2 servings

Per Serving
Calories 310 • Carbohydrates 11 g • Cholesterol 260 mg
Fat 12 g • Protein 42 g • Sodium 135 mg

Le Chardonnay

Mustard-Pepper Chicken with Herb Sauce

This dish is delicious served with mashed potatoes and green beans. The herb sauce may be made 1 day ahead, covered, and refrigerated.

Herb Sauce

½ tablespoon unsalted butter

2 shallots, coarsely chopped

3 large mushrooms, quartered

½ teaspoon freshly ground black pepper

½ cup dry white wine

3 fresh rosemary sprigs

3 fresh thyme sprigs

1 cup chicken stock (see page 225) or canned low-salt chicken broth

3 teaspoons freshly ground black pepper

4 boneless, skinless chicken breast halves

2 tablespoons Dijon mustard

½ tablespoon whole yellow mustard seeds

½ tablespoon butter

¼ teaspoon minced fresh thyme

To make the herb sauce: In a large, heavy skillet over medium-high heat, melt the butter. Add the shallots, mushrooms, and the pepper; sauté until the vegetables are lightly browned, about 8 minutes. Add the wine, raise the heat to high, and bring the liquid to a boil. Add the rosemary and thyme sprigs, reduce the heat to low, and simmer for 5 minutes. Add the stock or broth, raise the heat to high, and boil the liquid until it has reduced to ¾ cup, about 15 minutes. Strain through a fine-meshed sieve into a small saucepan.

Light a fire in a charcoal grill or preheat the broiler. Sprinkle the pepper over both sides of the chicken breasts. Grill the chicken over hot coals or

Le Chardonnay

under the broiler until opaque throughout, about 5 minutes on each side. Transfer to a baking sheet.

Preheat the broiler if necessary. In a small bowl, combine the Dijon mustard and the mustard seeds. Brush the mustard mixture over the tops of the chicken breasts and brown under the broiler for about 2 minutes.

Meanwhile, bring the herb sauce to a simmer. Add the minced thyme and whisk in the butter until melted.

Divide the chicken breasts between 2 plates and spoon some of the herb sauce around them; serve immediately.

Makes 2 servings

Per Serving
Calories 420 • Carbohydrates 9 g • Cholesterol 160 mg
Fat 15 g • Protein 58 g • Sodium 560 mg

Apple Fritters

1 cup unbleached all-purpose flour
1 tablespoon sugar
Pinch of salt
2 tablespoons peanut oil
¾ cup beer
1½ egg whites
2 Golden Delicious apples, peeled, cored, and cut into ¼-inch-thick slices
Sifted confectioners' sugar (optional)
Apricot Sauce (see page 229)
2 small scoops vanilla ice cream or frozen yogurt, optional

In a medium bowl, mix together the flour, sugar, salt, and peanut oil. Add the beer and stir until smooth. In a small bowl, whisk the egg whites until stiff peaks form; carefully fold into the fritter batter.

To a large, heavy pot or deep-fryer, add canola oil to a depth of 2 inches. Heat over medium-high heat to 375°F, or until almost smoking. Dip the apple slices into the fritter batter and carefully drop them into the hot oil in small batches. Cook, turning once, until deep golden, about 1 minute on each side. Remove each batch with a slotted spoon and drain on paper towels to absorb the excess oil. Transfer to a plate and dust with powdered sugar, if desired.

Spoon some of the apricot sauce onto 2 plates. Arrange the apple fritters on top of the sauce and top with a small scoop of vanilla ice cream or frozen yogurt, if you like. Serve immediately.

Makes 2 servings

Per Serving (without apricot sauce or ice cream or frozen yogurt)
Calories 440 • Carbohydrates 39 g • Cholesterol 0 mg
Fat 28 g • Protein 4 g • Sodium 110 mg

Le Chardonnay

New World Grill

New York, New York

Richard Barber and Katy Keck opened the New World Grill in 1993. Set in the World Wide Plaza in Manhattan, a residential and commerical development with a wonderful brick and stone plaza, the restaurant is a bright gazebolike structure on the southern end of the plaza.

Chef Katy Keck's menu offers simple, superbly prepared dishes with lively influences from Asia and the American Southwest. The intimate half-moon dining room wraps around a handsome bar and opens onto a pleasant terrace for alfresco dining. The following recipes were created by chef Katy Keck.

THE MENU
New World Grill

Grilled Pears with Field Greens, Stilton Cheese, and Toasted Walnuts

Asian Marinated Pork Tenderloin with Chili Lentils and Citrus Salsa

Tropical Fruit Soup

Serves Four

Grilled Pears with Field Greens, Stilton Cheese, and Toasted Walnuts

2 firm ripe pears, peeled, cored, and sliced
1 tablespoon vegetable oil for brushing
6 ounces mixed baby greens
⅓ cup Balsamic Vinaigrette (recipe follows)
4 teaspoons chopped walnuts, toasted (see page 232)
4 teaspoons crumbled Stilton or other blue cheese
Salt and freshly ground black pepper to taste

Light a fire in a charcoal grill or preheat a broiler. Gently brush the pear slices with vegetable oil and grill over hot coals or broil until lightly caramelized and slightly softened, 3 to 5 minutes. Remove from heat and let cool slightly.

In a medium bowl, toss the baby greens with the balsamic vinaigrette, walnuts, and Stilton cheese; season with salt and pepper.

In the center of 4 plates, arrange the greens in a tall pile and lean the pears against the greens.

Makes 4 servings

Per Serving
Calories 220 • Carbohydrates 16 g • Cholesterol less than 5 mg
Fat 17 g • Protein 2 g • Sodium 230 mg

Balsamic Vinaigrette

3 tablespoons balsamic vinegar
2 garlic cloves, minced
1 teaspoon minced shallot
1 teaspoon minced fresh parsley
½ teaspoon kosher salt
¼ teaspoon freshly ground black pepper
5 tablespoons olive oil

In a small bowl, combine the vinegar, garlic, shallots, parsley, salt, and pepper; set aside for 20 minutes. Whisk in the olive oil to make a vinaigrette.

Makes ½ cup

Per Serving
Calories 80 • Carbohydrates 2 g • Cholesterol 0 mg
Fat 8 g • Protein 0 g • Sodium 135 mg

Asian Marinated Pork Tenderloin with Chili Lentils and Citrus Salsa

3 tablespoons minced fresh cilantro

3 garlic cloves, minced

2 tablespoons soy sauce

2 tablespoons Asian sesame oil

4 teaspoons unseasoned rice vinegar

4 teaspoons molasses

4 teaspoons black bean–garlic paste (available in Asian markets)

4 teaspoons grated fresh ginger

¼ teaspoon freshly ground black pepper

Two 8-ounce pork tenderloins, trimmed of silver skin

Chili Lentils

1½ teaspoons olive oil

⅓ cup minced red onion

¼ cup chopped celery

¼ cup chopped red bell pepper

2 garlic cloves, minced

2 cups French green lentils

4 cups chicken stock (see page 225) or canned low-salt chicken broth

4½ teaspoons ancho chili powder or more to taste

2 teaspoons ground cumin

⅛ teaspoon cayenne pepper

⅛ teaspoon freshly ground black pepper

1 bay leaf

½ cup diced tomato

Citrus Salsa (recipe follows)

    In a large glass or ceramic bowl, stir together the cilantro, garlic, soy sauce, sesame oil, vinegar, molasses, black bean–garlic paste, ginger, and black pepper. Add the pork, turning to coat. Cover with plastic wrap and refrigerate for at least 2 hours or up to overnight, turning the pork occasionally in the marinade.

While the pork is marinating, make the lentils: In a large saucepan over medium heat, heat the olive oil. Add the onion, celery, bell pepper, and garlic; stir to coat. Add the lentils and sauté until the onion is translucent, about 7 minutes. Add the chicken stock or broth, chili powder, cumin, cayenne, pepper, and bay leaf. Bring the liquid to a boil, then reduce the heat to low and simmer for 20 minutes, adding water if necessary. Add the tomato and continue to cook 10 minutes longer, or until the lentils are tender. Remove and discard the bay leaf. Set aside.

Remove the pork tenderloins from the marinade and pat dry. Preheat the oven to 325°F. Place in a roasting pan and bake in the preheated oven until the pork registers 140°F. Remove from the oven, let rest for 10 minutes, then thinly slice.

Reheat the lentils. Place a mound of lentils in the center of each of 4 serving plates. Arrange the pork slices around the lentils and ring each plate with citrus salsa.

Makes 4 servings

Per Serving
Calories 600 • Carbohydrates 64 g • Cholesterol 65 mg
Fat 15 g • Protein 55 g • Sodium 660 mg

New World Grill

Citrus Salsa

1 small grapefruit
1 orange
¼ cup finely chopped red onion
¼ cup finely chopped red bell pepper
¼ cup finely chopped peeled and seeded cucumber
½ cup finely chopped fresh pineapple
1½ teaspoons minced seeded jalapeño chili
1 tablespoon unseasoned rice vinegar
1 tablespoon minced fresh cilantro

Section (see page 232) and chop the fruit. Transfer to a medium glass or ceramic bowl. Stir in all the remaining ingredients. Cover the salsa and refrigerate.

Makes about 2 cups

Per Serving
Calories 25 • Carbohydrates 6 g • Cholesterol 0 mg
Fat 0 g • Protein less than 1 g • Sodium 0 mg

New World Grill

Tropical Fruit Soup

2 cups water
2 tablespoons sugar
1 tablespoon grated orange zest
1 tablespoon grated lime zest
1 teaspoon grated fresh ginger
½ teaspoon Chinese five-spice powder
1 vanilla bean, split lengthwise, pulp scraped out and reserved
1 fresh mint sprig
4 coriander seeds
2 star anise pods
2 cloves
1 cup chopped pineapple
2 kiwis, peeled and chopped
1 papaya, peeled, seeded, and chopped
1 mango, peeled, pitted, and chopped
1 passion fruit, halved, scooped from shell, and chopped
4 or 6 scoops mango sorbet

In a small saucepan over medium heat, combine the water, sugar, orange and lime zests, ginger, five-spice powder, vanilla bean and pulp, mint, coriander seeds, star anise, and cloves; simmer for 10 minutes. Remove from heat and let infuse for 20 minutes; strain the infused liquid through a sieve.

In a medium bowl, combine the pineapple, kiwis, papaya, mango, and passion fruit; pour the infused liquid over. Cover and chill the fruit soup in the refrigerator.

Divide the fruit soup among 4 or 6 bowls and top with a scoop of mango sorbet.

Makes 4 to 6 servings

Per Serving
Calories 150 • Carbohydrates 36 g • Cholesterol 0 mg
Fat 1.5 g • Protein 2 g • Sodium 45 mg

Oritalia

San Francisco, California

Oritalia, a name derived from Oriental and Italian, is the inspiration of Nori and Kiku Yoshida. Their restaurant specializes in blending Asian flavors with Italian cuisine, a culinary style they pioneered when Oritalia opened in 1988. More than half of the restaurant's menu features dishes that blend the flavors and cooking styles of Italy, China, Korea, Japan, and Southeast Asia. Starting with the finest ingredients available, including organic produce grown in San Francisco neighborhood gardens, chef Bruce Hill's dishes capture the eye as well as the palate and balance East with West in flavor, texture, and presentation.

Oritalia's seasonal menu features a few signature dishes year-round. Small plates were introduced by Oritalia to enable diners to share a variety of dishes, tasting as little or as much as desired. This "grazing" concept is especially suited to today's lighter eating habits, as well as for pre- or post-theater dining. Pasta and a few "large plate" items are also offered. In a contemporary, casual setting that includes textured walls, papier mâché paintings, and lamps by an American glass artist, the Yoshidas regularly introduce new works of art to the forty-eight-seat restaurant.

The following recipes were created by chef Bruce Hill, formerly of Aqua and Stars, who has expanded Oritalia's menu by using seasonal exotic vegetables, adding seafood and "large plates," and introducing a new dessert menu.

THE MENU
Oritalia

Grilled Vegetable Salad with Soy-Ginger Dressing

Seafood Mu-Shu with Whole-Wheat Mandarin Pancakes

Miso-poached Salmon with Celery Root Purée, Baby Leeks, and Onions

Lemon Wintermint and Cherry Granita

Serves Four

Oritalia

Grilled Vegetable Salad with Soy-Ginger Dressing

Soy Ginger Dressing

1 cup chopped fresh ginger

¾ cup fresh lemon juice

¼ cup soy sauce

½ teaspoon balsamic vinegar

1 teaspoon minced garlic

½ cup canola oil

Salad

1 Japanese eggplant, cut into ¼-inch thick slices

Salt

1 zucchini, cut into ¼-inch-thick slices

1 yellow squash, cut into ⅛-inch-thick slices

1 red onion, cut into ⅛-inch dice

1 red bell pepper, quartered, seeded, and deribbed

2 large shiitake mushrooms, stemmed

2 teaspoons canola oil for brushing

4 handfuls mixed baby greens

To make the dressing: In a blender or food processor, purée the ginger, lemon juice, soy sauce, balsamic vinegar, and garlic for several seconds. With the motor running, slowly add the canola oil to make a dressing; set aside.

To make the salad: Place the eggplant slices on a baking sheet and salt them on both sides; top with a second baking sheet and a weight, and set aside for 1 hour.

Meanwhile, in a medium bowl, marinate the zucchini, squash, onion, red pepper, and mushrooms in the soy-ginger dressing for 45 minutes, tossing them every 10 minutes. Drain the vegetables and reserve the dressing.

Preheat the broiler or light a fire in a charcoal grill. Pat the flattened eggplant dry with paper towels and lightly brush the eggplant with canola oil. Broil the eggplant and marinated vegetables under the broiler, or place them in a grill basket or a grilling grid over hot coals, until crisp-tender, about 3 minutes on each side.

In a large bowl, toss the lettuce with some of the reserved dressing. Arrange the lettuce on 4 plates and top with the grilled vegetables. Lightly sprinkle the salad with some of the remaining dressing.

Makes 4 servings

Per Serving
Calories 370 • Carbohydrates 26 g • Cholesterol 0 mg
Fat 30 g • Protein 4 g • Sodium 1,050 mg

Seafood Mu-Shu with Whole-Wheat Mandarin Pancakes

Whole-Wheat Mandarin Pancakes

1 cup whole-wheat flour

1 cup unbleached all-purpose flour

½ teaspoon salt

¾ cup boiling water

1 tablespoon canola oil

3 teaspoons canola oil

8 ounces mixed shellfish and fish, such as shrimp, scallops, calamari,
   and firm-fleshed fish, diced

Salt and freshly ground black pepper to taste

1 tablespoon minced fresh ginger

1 tablespoon minced garlic

1 small yellow bell pepper, cored, seeded, and cut into julienne

4 large shiitake mushrooms, cut into julienne

¼ head Napa cabbage, cut into julienne

1 bunch green onions, cut into julienne

2 teaspoons soy sauce

Hoisin sauce for dipping

Chinese hot mustard for dipping

To make the pancakes: In a food processor, combine the whole-wheat flour, all-purpose flour, and salt. With the motor running, add the boiling water all at once and process until the mixture forms a ball. Or, combine the flours and salt in a medium bowl and stir the water in all at once, stirring until the dough pulls away from the sides of the bowl. Wrap the dough in plastic wrap and let rest at room temperature for 20 minutes or more.

On a lightly floured work surface, roll out the dough ⅛ inch thick. Cut twelve 2-inch circles of dough and brush 6 of them with canola oil. Place the remaining 6 circles of dough on top of the oiled dough circles. Roll each stack of 2 circles out to make 7-inch pancakes.

In a large dry skillet or sauté pan over medium heat, cook the pancakes for about 1 minute on each side, or until they peel apart easily. Separate the pancakes, transfer them to a plate, cover them with a dry towel, and set aside.

In a wok or large skillet over high heat, heat 1 teaspoon of the canola oil until almost smoking. Season the fish and shellfish with salt and pepper and stir-fry in the wok or skillet until the shrimp curls and turns pink and the other shellfish and fish become opaque, about 3 or 4 minutes. Remove from heat and set aside.

In the same wok or skillet over high heat, heat the remaining 2 teaspoons canola oil and stir-fry the ginger and garlic for 30 seconds. Stir in the yellow pepper and mushrooms and cook for 1 minute. Add the cabbage, green onions, soy sauce, and fish and shellfish; stir-fry for another 30 seconds. Serve immediately, with the warm pancakes, hoisin sauce, and Chinese mustard on the side.

Makes 4 servings

Per Serving (without dipping sauces)
Calories 300 • Carbohydrates 39 g • Cholesterol 80 mg
Fat 10 g • Protein 19 g • Sodium 620 mg

Oritalia

Miso-poached Salmon with Celery Root Purée, Baby Leeks, and Onions

Frizzled Leeks

2 cups julienned leeks (white part only)

Salt to taste

Celery Root Purée

2 cups finely diced peeled celery root

⅔ cup diced peeled potatoes, preferably Yukon gold potatoes

1 tablespoon unsalted butter

Salt and ground white pepper to taste

⅔ cup red pearl onions

⅔ cup yellow pearl onions

12 baby leeks or ramps (wild baby leeks)

3 cups chicken stock (see page 225) or canned low-salt chicken broth

½ cup yellow miso paste (available in Asian markets)

¼ cup mirin (available in Asian markets)

Four 6-ounce (3-by-3-by-1-inch) salmon fillets, skinned

2 tablespoons soy sauce

To make the frizzled leeks: Preheat the oven to 350°F. In a large pot of boiling salted water, blanch the leeks for 30 seconds. Drain the leeks and immediately immerse them in a large bowl of ice water. Drain well and squeeze dry between paper towels.

Spray a baking sheet with a thin coating of vegetable-oil cooking spray. Scatter the leeks evenly onto the sheet and spray them lightly with a little more cooking spray. Bake the leeks in the preheated oven for 15 minutes; turn them over gently with a spatula and bake for another 5 minutes, or until all sides are golden. Lightly salt the leeks, drain them on paper towels, and set aside.

To make the celery root purée: In a large pot of boiling salted water,

Oritalia

cook the celery root and potatoes, uncovered, until tender, about 15 to 20 minutes. In a blender or food processor, blend the celery root, potatoes, and butter until very smooth. Strain the purée through a medium-meshed sieve, pushing the mixture through with the back of a wooden spoon. Season with salt and pepper. Place the purée in a pastry bag without a tip and keep warm in a 200°F oven until ready to serve.

Place the red and yellow pearl onions in boiling water to cover for 10 seconds. Drain, let cool, and trim the top and bottom. Slip off the skin and cut an X in the root end of each onion. In a saucepan over medium heat, simmer the pearl onions, leeks or ramps, and stock or broth until the onions are tender. Drain the vegetables and reserve them and the stock or broth.

In a 12-inch skillet or sauté pan over medium heat, combine the reserved stock or broth, the miso paste, mirin, and soy sauce; bring to a boil, stirring to break up any lumps. Remove from heat and add the salmon fillets and reserved vegetables. Return the skillet or pan to low heat, cover, and gently poach until the salmon is opaque on the outside but slightly translucent within, about 4 minutes; make sure the liquid does not come to a boil.

Arrange the vegetables around the outer edge of 4 plates. Pipe 4-inch disks of celery root purée in the center of each plate. Using a slotted spatula, remove the salmon fillets from the cooking liquid and place on top of the celery root purée disks. Taste the poaching liquid for seasoning and add some hot water if it is too salty. Spoon 3 tablespoons of poaching liquid over each salmon fillet, and top each fillet with a tall stack of frizzled leeks.

Makes 4 servings

Per Serving
Calories 520 • Carbohydrates 39 g • Cholesterol 105 mg
Fat 17 g • Protein 53 g • Sodium 670 mg

Oritalia

Lemon Wintermint and Cherry Granita

1 cup boiling water
⅓ cup Republic of Tea Lemon Wintermint tea or other mint tea
1½ pounds (4 cups) fresh Bing cherries, pitted
⅓ cup plus 2 tablespoons sugar
2 tablespoons fresh lemon juice
Fresh mint sprigs for garnish

In a teapot or saucepan, pour the boiling water over the tea leaves; cover and let steep for 5 minutes. Strain and pour the tea into a blender or food processor. Add the cherries, sugar, and lemon juice and blend until smooth.

Pour the liquid through a fine-meshed sieve to remove the cherry skins and any remaining tea leaves. Pour the liquid into a large, shallow metal pan and freeze for 6 hours or more.

To serve, scrape the frozen granita into shavings with a spoon and place the shavings in 4 serving glasses. Garnish with a sprig of mint and serve immediately.

Makes 4 servings

Per Serving
Calories 200 • Carbohydrates 49 g • Cholesterol 0 mg
Fat 1.5 g • Protein 2 g • Sodium 0 mg

Oritalia

The Peaks at Telluride
The Legends of Telluride
Telluride, Colorado

Surrrounded by the peaks of Colorado's San Juan Mountains, The Peaks at Telluride offers skiing at the renowned Telluride ski area, year-round recreational activities, and a world-class spa. During the winter, resort guests enjoy easy access to more than one thousand acres of ski terrain, and during the rest of the year they can enjoy hiking, mountain biking, whitewater rafting, fly fishing, horseback riding, golf, and tennis. Nearby annual festivals include the Telluride Film Festival, Telluride Bluegrass Festival, Jazz Celebration, Chamber Music Festival, Wine Festival, Balloon Festival, and the Telluride Bicycle Classic. The Peaks has received the Four-Diamond Award from the American Automobile Association.

The Spa at The Peaks, one of North America's largest spas, offers more than an acre of treatment rooms and fitness facilities. By adapting Native American rituals to its programs and treatments and using products indigenous to Colorado, the Spa offers a unique opportunity for relaxation and rejuvenation.

When dining at The Legends, health-conscious guests savor regional delights. Peaks Performance Cuisine, designed by spa director Gayle Moeller, presents a selection of energy boosting, low-fat dishes that make the most of local produce, creating a healthful cuisine with regional flair. The Legends' menu also features Ranchlands Cuisine, classic American dishes with a Colorado accent. The Southwest design of the 130-seat dining room includes a rough-hewn wood-beam ceiling, plastered walls, western textiles, and a collage of musical instruments. Weather permitting, an outdoor brick-paved sun deck provides additional seating and overlooks some of the most spectacular country in the Rocky Mountains. The following recipes were created by executive chef Robert Kowalske.

THE MENU
The Legends of Telluride

Appetizer Pizzas

Shrimp and Corn Chowder

Grilled Vegetable Casseroles with Red Pepper Confit

Warm Asparagus Salad with Field Lettuces and Yellow Tomato Vinaigrette

Reduced-Fat Cheesecake

Serves Two

Appetizer Pizzas

Dough
1¼ teaspoons (½ package) active dry yeast
½ teaspoon salt
¼ teaspoon sugar
1 to 1¼ cups unbleached all-purpose flour
½ cup hot (120°F) water

Topping
1 tablespoon olive oil
1 onion, cut into julienne
¼ cup pesto (see page 230)
2 Roma (plum) tomatoes, thinly sliced
⅔ cup julienned Portobello mushroom
½ cup (2 ounces) grated Asiago cheese

To make the dough: In a large bowl, stir together the yeast, salt, sugar, and ½ cup of the flour. Gradually stir in the water and mix well; gradually add more of the remaining flour until the dough pulls away from the sides of the bowl. On a lightly floured work surface, knead the dough for 8 to 10 minutes. Add flour, if necessary, to keep the dough from sticking.

Transfer the dough to a lightly oiled medium bowl. Cover the bowl and let the dough rise until doubled in size, about 1 hour. When the dough has risen, place it on a lightly floured surface, divide in half, and form into 2 balls. Cover with a towel and let rise for 15 to 20 minutes. Preheat the oven to 350°F.

Meanwhile, to make the topping: In a medium skillet or sauté pan over low heat, heat the olive oil and cook the onion, stirring occasionally, until it browns, about 20 minutes; set the onions aside.

Coat a baking sheet with olive oil and sprinkle with cornmeal. Turn the dough out onto a lightly floured surface and roll out, or stretch the dough

The Legends of Telluride

with your hands, to make two 6-inch rounds. Spread the pesto over the dough and layer with the tomatoes, onions, and mushrooms. Sprinkle the pizzas with the cheese and transfer to the prepared baking sheet. Bake in the preheated oven for 9 minutes, or until the crust is browned and crisp on the bottom.

Makes two 6-inch pizzas

Per Serving
Calories 410 • Carbohydrates 22 g • Cholesterol 35 mg
Fat 29 g • Protein 17 g • Sodium 830 mg

The Legends of Telluride

Shrimp and Corn Chowder

1 red bell pepper, roasted, peeled, seeded, and chopped (see page XX)
1 cup chopped onion
1 garlic clove, minced
1 cup fresh corn kernels
1 cup low-fat (1 percent) milk
¾ teaspoon cornstarch
2 tablespoons water
Salt to taste
8 ounces medium shrimp, peeled
1 tablespoon shredded fresh basil

Coat a nonstick skillet or sauté pan with vegetable-oil spray, heat over medium heat, and sauté the onion and garlic until translucent, about 5 minutes. Add the onion, garlic, and corn kernels to a blender or food processor and blend for 15 seconds. Transfer the corn mixture to a large saucepan over medium heat. Stir in ½ cup of the milk and cook the soup for 15 minutes, stirring constantly. Stir in the remaining milk, cover, and reduce the heat to low; cook for 10 more minutes.

Strain the soup through a fine-meshed sieve, pressing with the back of a spoon to extract the liquids. Discard the pulp and return the soup to the saucepan. In a small bowl, stir together the cornstarch and water; stir the mixture into the soup. Add salt, raise the heat to high, and bring the soup to a boil. Reduce the heat to low and simmer until the soup has thickened, stirring frequently. Add the shrimp and cook for 3 to 5 minutes, or until the shrimp turns pink. Add the basil and red pepper and serve.

Makes 2 servings

Per Serving
Calories 180 • Carbohydrates 20 g • Cholesterol 140 mg
Fat 2.5 g • Protein 20 g • Sodium 220 mg

Grilled Vegetable Casseroles with Red Pepper Confit

In these casseroles, grilled vegetables and caramelized onions are layered with quinoa, a South American grain high in protein.

1 cup quinoa
2 cups water
2 red bell peppers
1 small zucchini, thinly sliced
1 small yellow squash, thinly sliced
2 tablespoons olive oil
1 red onion, finely chopped
3 small red potatoes, sliced ¼ inch thick and blanched for 1 minute
½ bunch spinach, stemmed and well washed
½ butternut squash, peeled and thinly sliced
10 shiitake mushrooms, stemmed
½ tablespoon minced garlic
½ tablespoon minced mixed fresh oregano and thyme
Salt and freshly ground black pepper to taste
Red Pepper Confit (recipe follows)

Light a fire in a charcoal grill. While the coals are heating, bring the water to a boil in a medium saucepan. Add the quinoa, cover, reduce the heat to low, and simmer for 12 to 15 minutes, or until all the water is absorbed.

When the coals are hot, place the red peppers on the grill and cook, turning them to blacken the skin evenly. Transfer from the grill to a paper or plastic bag, close the bag, and let cool for 15 minutes. Peel off the blackened skin and seed the pepper. Set aside.

In a medium bowl, combine the zucchini, yellow squash, and 1 tablespoon of the olive oil; mix until the vegetables are well coated. Place the zucchini and yellow squash in a hinged wire basket or on a grilling grid and grill, turning once, until the squash are crisp-tender, about 2 minutes on each side.

The Legends of Telluride

In a skillet or sauté pan over medium heat, heat the remaining 1 tablespoon of olive oil and sauté the onion, stirring occasionally, until it is browned, about 20 minutes.

Preheat the oven to 350°F. Cut parchment paper or waxed paper to fit the bottom of 2 individual casserole dishes. Spray the bottom and inner sides of the casserole dishes with vegetable oil spray. Lay the parchment or waxed paper into the casseroles and spray the paper again. Overlap the potato slices in the bottom of each casserole to make a spiral shape. Add a layer of yellow squash and sprinkle with salt and pepper to taste. Layer with the spinach, then the onion, garlic, herbs, and mushrooms. Spread the quinoa over the mushrooms and top with layers of zucchini, butternut squash, and red pepper. Place the casseroles on a baking sheet, cover them with aluminum foil, and bake in the preheated oven for 1 hour. Serve with red pepper confit.

Makes 2 servings

Per Serving (without red pepper confit)
Calories 660 • Carbohydrates 110 g • Cholesterol 0 mg
Fat 20 g • Protein 20 g • Sodium 110 mg

Red Pepper Confit

1 red bell pepper, seeded, deribbed, and cut into julienne
¾ cup dry white wine
3 tablespoons sugar
Juice of 3 limes

In a small saucepan over high heat, combine all of the ingredients and bring to a boil. Reduce the heat and simmer for 15 or 20 minutes, or until all the liquid has disappeared.

Makes about ½ cup

Per Serving
Calories 30 • Carbohydrates 6 g • Cholesterol 0 mg
Fat 0 g • Protein 0 g • Sodium 0 mg

The Legends of Telluride

Warm Asparagus Salad with Field Lettuces and Yellow Tomato Vinaigrette

1 tablespoon olive oil

1 teaspoon red wine vinegar

Salt and freshly ground black pepper to taste

12 tender asparagus spears, ends trimmed, cut into 4½-inch pieces

4 shiitake mushrooms, stemmed

1 Roma (plum) tomato, seeded and cut into ¼-inch dice

½ small onion, finely chopped

Juice of ½ lemon

Juice of ½ lime

2 handfuls baby greens

Yellow Tomato Vinaigrette (recipe follows)

Light a fire in a charcoal grill or preheat a gas grill. While the coals are heating, in a medium bowl, whisk together the olive oil, vinegar, salt, and pepper to make a vinaigrette. Add the asparagus pieces and coat them with the vinaigrette; set aside.

When the coals are medium hot, grill the mushrooms for 3 minutes, remove from heat, and cut into ¼-inch dice. In a medium bowl, combine the tomato, mushrooms, onion, lemon juice, lime juice, and salt and pepper to taste; set aside.

Place the asparagus pieces in a grill basket or on a grilling grid and grill over hot coals until bright green, about 2 minutes on each side.

Arrange the lettuce and grilled asparagus on 2 plates. Spoon some of the tomato-mushroom mixture over the asparagus and sprinkle with the yellow tomato vinaigrette.

Makes 2 servings

Per Serving (without yellow tomato vinaigrette)
Calories 130 • Carbohydrates 16 g • Cholesterol 0 mg
Fat 7 g • Protein 4 g • Sodium 20 mg

Yellow Tomato Vinaigrette

½ tablespoon Dijon mustard

2 yellow tomatoes, peeled, seeded, and diced

1 shallot, minced

1 garlic clove, minced

1 tablespoon dry white wine

½ teaspoon white wine vinegar

Juice of ½ lemon

1 tablespoon water

Salt and freshly ground black pepper to taste

In a small bowl, whisk together all the ingredients.

Per Serving
Calories 45 • Carbohydrates 9 g • Cholesterol 25 mg
Fat 1 g • Protein 2 g • Sodium 105 mg

Reduced-Fat Cheesecake

Blueberry cake takes the place of a graham cracker crust for this cheesecake. The blueberry cake is also delicious served by itself.

Cheesecake

1 pound non-fat cream cheese at room temperature

¾ cup sugar

1 tablespoon vanilla extract

1 cup egg whites (about 6 whites)

½ teaspoon grated lemon zest

1 tablespoon fresh lemon juice

2 tablespoons flour

1 egg yolk

1 tablespoon cornstarch

Blueberry Cake Base

½ cup vegetable oil

1¼ cups sugar

1 tablespoon vanilla extract

½ cup low-fat (1 percent) milk

½ cup non-fat plain yogurt

2½ cups unbleached all-purpose flour

1¼ teaspoons baking soda

5 egg whites

¼ teaspoon cream of tartar

2½ cups fresh or frozen blueberries

¼ cup seedless raspberry jam for coating

To make the cheesecake: Preheat the oven to 350°F. Grease and flour a 10-inch cake pan with a removable bottom. In a large bowl, beat together the cream cheese and sugar until fluffy. Beat in the vanilla and egg whites until well blended. Stir in the lemon zest and juice, flour, egg yolk, and cornstarch. Pour the batter into the prepared pan. Place the pan in a shallow baking dish and fill the dish with water to halfway up the sides of the pie pan.

Bake in the preheated oven for 40 to 50 minutes, or until a toothpick inserted in the center comes out almost clean. Do not overbake; the cheesecake will firm as it cools. Let cool to room temperature on a wire rack, then unmold. Refrigerate for several hours or overnight.

To make the blueberry cake base: Preheat the oven to 350°F. Grease and flour a 10-inch cake pan. In a large bowl, stir together the oil, sugar, vanilla, milk, and yogurt until thoroughly blended. Sift the flour and baking soda together and stir into the yogurt mixture.

In a large bowl, whisk the egg whites and cream of tartar until soft peaks form. Gently fold the egg whites, then the blueberries, into the batter until blended. Pour the batter into the prepared cake pan. Bake in the preheated oven for 1 hour, or until a knife inserted in the center comes out clean. Let cool to room temperature on a wire rack, then unmold. Refrigerate the blueberry cake until chilled.

Slice the blueberry cake into 2 layers using a long serrated knife. Place one of the layers on a 10-inch cardboard cake circle and spread with a thin layer of raspberry jam; reserve the other layer for another use. Cover another 10-inch cardboard circle with sugar and place the cheesecake on top. Invert the blueberry cake base on top of the cheesecake, then, holding the two together, invert them and the cardboard circles. Remove the top cardboard circle and spread a thin layer of raspberry jam on the sides of the cheesecake.

Makes one 10-inch cheesecake

Per Serving
Calories 230 • Carbohydrates 35 g • Cholesterol 25 mg
Fat 5 g • Protein 10 g • Sodium 350 mg

The Legends of Telluride

Quadrangle Grille

Dallas, Texas

Quadrangle Grille, a casually upscale American-style grill in the heart of Dallas, was opened in 1989 by Tom Stark. Its proximity to Meyerson Symphony Hall, the Dallas Museum of Art, Dallas Theater Center, and Reunion Arena makes it a natural dining destination before or after theater, concert, or sporting events. Comfortable and contemporary, the restaurant's decor is highlighted by a 48-by-7-foot mural depicting a colorful day in the life of the grill. Quadrangle's large outdoor patio is surrounded by lush land-scaping, fountains, and large shade trees. Colorful market umbrellas dot the patio for shaded dining.

Tom Stark describes Quadrangle's eclectic menu as "honest and sensible, but with a creative twist." The kitchen features grilled fish, seafood, chicken, pork, beef, and vegetables. A large selection of pizzas, pastas, salads, and daily specials is offered during lunch and dinner, and a Late Night Menu for Late Night People is served Thursday through Saturday. The all-American wine list features wines from California, Washington, and Texas. The following recipes were created by chef Wayne Reynolds.

Quadrangle Grille

THE MENU
Quadrangle Grille

Watercress and Vegetable Soup

Fresh Pasta with Grilled Vegetables and Grilled-Vegetable Sauce

Strawberry-Yogurt Cheesecake

Serves Four

Quadrangle Grille

Watercress and Vegetable Soup

2 tablespoons olive oil

1 leek, white part only, finely chopped

1 zucchini, diced

1 yellow squash, diced

1 carrot, peeled and diced

1 celery stalk, chopped

2 tablespoons minced fresh chives

⅔ cup canned garbanzo beans, drained

4½ cups chicken stock (see page 225) or
   canned low-salt chicken broth, or more as needed

1 teaspoon minced fresh thyme

3 cups packed watercress sprigs

In a large sauté pan or skillet over medium heat, heat the olive oil and sauté the leek, zucchini, yellow squash, carrot, celery, chives, and garbanzo beans until tender, about 7 minutes. Add the 4½ cups stock or broth and the thyme and simmer for 10 minutes, then add the watercress and cook until wilted. Transfer the soup to a blender or food processor and purée until smooth, in batches if necessary. If the soup is too thick, add more stock or broth. Heat briefly and serve in shallow soup bowls.

Makes 4 servings

Per Serving
Calories 170 • Carbohydrates 18 g • Cholesterol 0 mg
Fat 8 g • Protein 7 g • Sodium 200 mg

Quadrangle Grille

Fresh Pasta with Grilled Vegetables and Grilled-Vegetable Sauce

Marinade

1½ teaspoons minced fresh oregano

1½ teaspoons minced fresh thyme

1½ teaspoons minced fresh basil

½ teaspoon freshly ground black pepper

½ teaspoon kosher salt

2 tablespoons sugar

2 tablespoons red wine vinegar

1 teaspoon Dijon mustard

1 cup olive oil

1 eggplant

2 zucchini

2 yellow squash

2 yellow onions

2 carrots, peeled

2 *each* red and green bell peppers, halved lengthwise,
  seeded, and deribbed

6 tomatoes, cut into ¼-inch-thick crosswise slices

8 ounces fresh fettuccine

1 pound fresh tomatoes, seeded and chopped

In a large bowl, combine all the marinade ingredients. Cut the eggplant, zucchini, squash, onions, and carrots into ¼-inch-thick lengthwise slices. Cut the peppers into 1-inch-wide strips. Marinate the vegetables for about 3 hours, tossing several times. Drain the vegetables and reserve the marinade.

Light a fire in a charcoal grill or preheat a broiler. Place the vegetables in a grill basket or on a grilling grid and cook them over hot coals until crisp-tender, about 3 minutes on each side. Or, broil the vegetables 3 inches from

Quadrangle Grille

the heating element for about 3 minutes on each side. Remove from heat and let cool. Cut all the vegetables into ½-inch-long pieces.

In a large pot of boiling salted water, cook the pasta until al dente, about 2 minutes; drain.

In a large bowl, toss together the vegetables, reserved marinade, and pasta. Serve at once.

Makes 4 servings

Per Serving
Calories 840 • Carbohydrates 76 g • Cholesterol 40 mg
Fat 57 g • Protein 13 g • Sodium 540 mg

Strawberry-Yogurt Cheesecake

Crust

1½ cups crushed oat bran cereal

One 6-ounce can thawed frozen apple juice concentrate

1 teaspoon ground cinnamon

Filling

2 eggs, lightly beaten

1½ cups nonfat plain yogurt

⅓ cup sugar

2 tablespoons fresh strawberry juice or purée

½ teaspoon vanilla extract

2 cups fresh strawberries, hulled and halved

Preheat the oven to 350°F. In a small bowl, combine the oat bran cereal, apple juice concentrate, and cinnamon until well blended. Using the back of a spoon, press the mixture into the bottom and sides of a 9-inch glass pie pan.

In a medium bowl, combine the eggs, yogurt, sugar, strawberry juice or purée, and vanilla until well blended and smooth. Pour the filling into the prepared crust and place the pan on a baking sheet. Bake until set, about 25 to 30 minutes.

Let the the cheesecake cool in the pan on a wire rack, then refrigerate until chilled, at least 2 hours. Arrange the strawberry halves, cut-side down, on top.

Makes 8 servings

Per Serving
Calories 150 • Carbohydrates 29 g • Cholesterol 55 mg
Fat 2 g • Protein 6 g • Sodium 120 mg

Quail Lodge Resort & Golf Club
The Covey Restaurant

Carmel, California

Quail Lodge Resort and Golf Club is the realized dream of proprietor Edgar Haber. He has transformed a former dairy farm into a world-class resort located near California's Big Sur coastline and minutes away from Carmel, Pebble Beach, and Monterey. Remaining sensitive to the environment of Carmel Valley, the resort is set on 245 beautifully landscaped acres, with an additional six hundred acres of nature preserve.

Quail Lodge has received the prestigious Mobil Travel Guide's Five-Star designation, an award it has won for nineteen years. Its recreational facilities include a championship eighteen-hole golf course, two swimming pools, four tennis courts, a croquet court, and trails for jogging and bicycling. Guest accommodations are located in country-style cottages nestled throughout the property, most with a view of at least one of the resort's ten lakes.

The Covey Restaurant at Quail Lodge provides an exceptional dining experience and is a winner of the prestigious DiRoNa Award. Chef Bob Williamson's menu blends culinary excellence with disciplined artistic freedom. European training and years of experience have enabled Williamson to master the fine art of combining foods. He is noted for creating dinners to set off a particular wine, special theme dinners, and variations of a favorite dish to please a guest. Williamson's favorite ingredients include herbs grown in the Quail Lodge greenhouse and courtyard herb garden and fresh produce from the fields of Carmel Valley and nearby Salinas Valley, known as "the salad bowl of the nation." The Covey's extensive wine list emphasizes California and Monterey County wines and is a consistent winner of *The Wine Spectator's* Award of Excellence. The following recipes were created by chef Robert Williamson.

The Covey Restaurant

THE MENU
The Covey Restaurant

Artichoke Hors d'Oeuvre with Fennel and Garbanzo Bean Dip

Tomato Bisque with Corn Relish

Tossed Greens and Rice Sticks with Southeast Asian Dressing

Rock Shrimp, Mango, and Coconut Milk Curry

Sunburst Sorbet

Serves Four

Artichoke Hors d'Oeuvre with Fennel and Garbanzo Bean Dip

If you are preparing this dish ahead of time it may be refrigerated, but let it come to room temperature before serving.

1 small fennel bulb
2 tablespoons olive oil or more as needed
2 tablespoons fresh lemon juice or more as needed,
   plus juice of ½ lemon in a large bowl of water
4 artichokes
Salt to taste
⅓ cup canned garbanzo beans with liquid
Freshly ground black pepper and cayenne pepper to taste

Slice the bottom and top off the fennel bulb and remove the tough outer leaves. Halve the bulb, cut out the core, and slice crosswise into ½-inch-thick slices. In a nonaluminum saucepan with a tight-fitting lid over very low heat, combine the fennel, 2 tablespoons olive oil, and 2 tablespoons lemon juice and cook for 20 minutes.

Meanwhile, prepare the artichokes: Slice the stems off the artichokes. Snap off the first few small leaves. Trim any dark green parts from the bottom. Cut off the tips of the leaves, if you wish. Quarter the artichokes and cut each quarter in half. Scoop out the chokes with a spoon and place the artichokes in the lemon water as you work to prevent discoloration.

Drain the artichokes and place in the saucepan on top of the fennel. Add more oil or lemon juice, if you wish. Season with salt and cover the pan tightly. Cook over low heat until the artichokes are tender, about 25 to 30 minutes. Add a little water if necessary to keep them moist.

Arrange the cooked artichokes on a serving tray; reserve the fennel. Let the artichokes cool to room temperature while making the dip.

The Covey Restaurant

Place the cooked fennel in a blender or food processor and purée. Add the garbanzo beans and enough of their liquid to make a purée of dipping consistency. Season with salt, pepper, and cayenne. Spoon the dip into a small bowl and place it in the center of the artichoke tray.

Makes 4 servings

Per Serving
Calories 260 • Carbohydrates 22 g • Cholesterol 0 mg
Fat 3 g • Protein 6 g • Sodium 200 mg

The Covey Restaurant

Tomato Bisque with Corn Relish

2 tablespoons olive oil
1 small onion, chopped
1 garlic clove, crushed
⅓ cup tomato paste
⅔ cup dry white wine
3 pounds ripe tomatoes, seeded and chopped
1⅓ cups chicken stock (see page 225) or canned low-salt chicken broth
Bouquet garni: 6 parsley stems, 3 oregano stems, and a bayleaf
   tied with cotton string
Salt, freshly ground black pepper, and Worcestershire sauce to taste
2 egg yolks
½ cup half-and-half
Corn Relish (recipe follows)

In a large, heavy saucepan over medium heat, heat the olive oil and sauté the onion and garlic until they are translucent, 3 to 4 minutes. Add the tomato paste and cook for 1 to 2 minutes, stirring constantly. Add the white wine, tomatoes, stock or broth, and bouquet garni. Bring to a boil, then reduce the heat and simmer for 20 to 25 minutes.

Remove from heat, strain the soup through a sieve, and return it to the saucepan over high heat. Season with salt, pepper, and Worcestershire sauce.

In a medium bowl, whisk together the egg yolks and half-and-half; pour this mixture into the soup, stirring constantly. Gently heat the soup until it thickens; be very careful to not allow it to boil or the mixture will curdle.

Place a mound of corn relish in the center of each of 4 shallow soup bowls and ladle in the tomato bisque.

Makes 4 servings

Per Serving (without corn relish)
Calories 260 • Carbohydrates 25 g • Cholesterol 120 mg
Fat 15 g • Protein 8 g • Sodium 250 mg

Corn Relish

3 ears white corn
1 small red onion
1 green bell pepper
3 tablespoons minced fresh basil
1 tablespoon fresh lemon juice
2 tablespoons extra-virgin olive oil
1 jalapeño chili, seeded and minced (optional)
Salt and freshly ground black pepper to taste

Using a sharp knife, cut the corn kernels from the cobs. In a large pot of boiling water, cook the corn kernels for 5 minutes, or until crisp-tender. Remove from heat, drain, and rinse under cold water.

In a medium bowl, stir together the corn, onion, bell pepper, basil, lemon juice, olive oil, and optional jalapeño. Season with salt and pepper.

Per Serving
Calories 45 • Carbohydrates 5 g • Cholesterol 0 mg
Fat 2.5 g • Protein 1 g • Sodium 5 mg

The Covey Restaurant

Tossed Greens and Rice Sticks with Southeast Asian Dressing

Canola oil for frying

4 small handfuls rice stick noodles (available at Asian markets)

4 handfuls mixed baby lettuces

Southeast Asian Dressing

¼ cup Thai fish sauce (available at Asian markets)

1 cup very hot water

¼ cup unseasoned rice vinegar

2 tablespoons sugar

Tabasco sauce to taste

Pour 2 inches of canola oil in a wok or heavy skillet. Heat the oil to 375°F, or until almost smoking. Drop in half of the rice noodles. Turn the noodles quickly with 2 spoons until they become crisp and golden. Using a slotted spoon, remove and drain on paper towels. Repeat to fry the remaining noodles.

To make the dressing: Whisk all the ingredients together in a small bowl.

Place the lettuce in a large bowl and toss with the dressing. Divide the salad among 4 plates and top with the fried rice stick noodles.

Makes 4 servings

Per Serving
Calories 110 • Carbohydrates 19 g • Cholesterol 0 mg
Fat 2.5 g • Protein 3 g • Sodium 2,470 mg

The Covey Restaurant

Rock Shrimp, Mango, and Coconut Milk Curry

2 ripe mangoes, peeled and sliced

Freshly ground black pepper to taste

Sugar to taste

2 tablespoons unsalted butter

1 shallot, minced

1 garlic clove, minced

1 teaspoon flour

1 tablespoon curry powder

1 tablespoon dry white wine

One 14-ounce can Thai coconut milk

½ tablespoon fresh lemon juice

Salt to taste

2 tablespoons clarified butter (see page 230)

8 ounces rock shrimp, peeled and deveined

Chive flower petals and minced fresh chives for garnish

Preheat the broiler. Arrange the mango slices in a single layer on an ovenproof tray and season with pepper and sugar. Place under the broiler for 1 to 2 minutes, or until lightly glazed. Set aside.

In a saucepan over medium heat, melt the butter and sauté the shallot and garlic for 1 to 2 minutes. In a small bowl, mix together the flour and curry powder. Stir this mixture and the white wine into the shallot mixture.

Pour off 2 or 3 tablespoons of the clear liquid from the coconut milk and reserve. Add the rest of the coconut milk to the curry and stir well. Raise the heat to high and bring the liquid to a boil; cook to reduce the liquid by half. Stir in the lemon juice and season with salt and pepper.

In a medium skillet or sauté pan over medium heat, heat the clarified butter and sauté the shrimp for 2 to 3 minutes, or until the shrimp turn pink.

The Covey Restaurant

Adjust the seasoning and then the curry with some of the reserved coconut liquid, if necessary.

Arrange the mango in a flower pattern on each of 4 plates and spoon the curried shrimp into the centers. Sprinkle with chive petals and chives.

Makes 4 servings

Per Serving
Calories 450 • Carbohydrates 25 g • Cholesterol 110 mg
Fat 36 g • Protein 12 g • Sodium 170 mg

The Covey Restaurant

Sunburst Sorbet

A beautiful, refreshing dessert: raspberry sorbet surrounded by orange caramel-topped oranges and strawberries.

Raspberry Sorbet

1 basket fresh raspberries, or one 10-ounce package thawed
    frozen unsweetened raspberries
1 cup sugar
1 cup water
Juice of 1 lemon

4 oranges, peeled and sectioned (see page 232)
8 large fresh strawberries, hulled and quartered
Orange Caramel (recipe follows)
Mint leaves or julienned orange zest for garnish

To make the raspberry sorbet: In a blender or food processor, purée the raspberries; you should have 1½ cups purée. In a small saucepan over high heat, bring the water and sugar to a boil; remove from heat and let cool. Stir in the raspberry purée and lemon juice. Freeze in an ice cream freezer according to the manufacturer's directions.

Place a rounded scoop of raspberry sorbet in the center of each of 4 plates and surround with orange sections and strawberries in a sunburst design. Drizzle the fruit with some of the orange caramel and garnish with mint leaves or orange zest.

Makes 12 servings

Per Serving
Calories 100 • Carbohydrates 26 g • Cholesterol 0 mg
Fat 0 g • Protein 0 g • Sodium 0 mg

The Covey Restaurant

Orange Caramel

½ cup sugar
½ cup water
½ cup fresh orange juice or more as needed
½ to ¾ cup Grand Marnier

In a small, heavy saucepan over high heat, cook the sugar and water until the sugar turns a light amber. Immediately remove from heat and stir in the orange juice and Grand Marnier. Add more orange juice if the orange caramel is too thick. Store in an airtight jar in the refrigerator.

Makes about 1¾ cup

Per Serving
Calories 30 • Carbohydrates 6 g • Cholesterol 0 mg
Fat 0 g • Protein 0 g • Sodium 0 mg

Rancho Bernardo Inn
El Bizcocho Restaurant

San Diego, California

The Rancho Bernardo Inn is a luxurious tennis and golf resort set on 265 acres of lushly landscaped grounds in the San Pasqual Mountains thirty miles from San Diego. The family-owned inn, which has received the prestigious Four-Star Award from the Mobil Travel Guide, is built in the style of a luxurious early California country home. Red-tiled roofs, whitewashed stucco walls, fountains, period antiques, and commissioned historical art help to recapture a bygone era in California.

With its year-round ideal climate, Rancho Bernardo offers facilities for sports, play, and relaxation, including a state-of-the-art fitness center, championship golf courses, a golf school, twelve tennis courts, and swimming pools. Rancho Bernardo is located near three California missions, ocean beaches, and acres of commercial flower gardens and avocado groves.

El Bizcocho restaurant features classic French dishes adapted to the lighter cooking style of California. El Bizcocho is a winner of the Mobil Three-Star Award and has received the prestigious DiRoNa award since 1992. Chef Thomas Dowling's contemporary cooking highlights California seafood and produce. There is a nightly performance of piano music in the romantic mission-style dining room. The wine list, including wines from over seven hundred wineries and an extensive selection of rare cognacs and liqueurs, has been honored with *The Wine Spectator's* Best of Award of Excellence. The following recipes were created by chef Thomas B. Dowling.

THE MENU
El Bizcocho Restaurant

Baked Halibut with Leeks and Mustard Sauce

Roasted Eggplant Soup

Grilled Duck Breast with Oranges and Basil

Apple Tart with Cinnamon and Ginger Infusion

Serves Four

Baked Halibut with Leeks and Mustard Sauce

Four 4-ounce halibut fillets
Salt and freshly ground black pepper to taste
3 tablespoons sun-dried tomato purée

Topping
2 tablespoons butter
⅔ cup diced leek (white part only)
⅓ cup dried white bread crumbs
2 teaspoons minced fresh lemon thyme
⅛ teaspoon salt
⅛ teaspoon ground white pepper

Mustard Sauce
2 tablespoons non-fat milk
6 tablespoons Pommery or Dijon mustard
1 bunch fresh dill sprigs, minced
Salt and freshly ground black pepper to taste

Preheat the oven to 325°F. Coat a baking dish with olive oil and add the fillets, season with salt and pepper, and coat the tops with the tomato purée.

To make the topping: In a small skillet or sauté pan over medium heat, melt the butter and sauté the leek until soft but not browned. In a medium bowl, stir together the leek and remaining ingredients; cover the fillets with the topping. Bake in the preheated oven for 12 minutes, or until the fish is opaque throughout.

While the fish is baking, prepare the mustard sauce: In a small saucepan over medium heat, stir together all the ingredients until thoroughly blended and heated through. Set aside and keep warm.

To serve, carefully transfer the fillets to 4 warmed plates, spoon 2 tablespoons of warm mustard sauce around each fillet and serve at once.

Makes 4 servings

Per Serving
Calories 270 • Carbohydrates 14 g • Cholesterol 55 mg
Fat 11 g • Protein 26 g • Sodium 900 mg

Roasted Eggplant Soup

Low in calories and fat, eggplants are high in fiber and carbohydrates.

Soup

4 large globe eggplants

½ cup olive oil

¼ cup sesame oil

1 onion, diced

1 leek, sliced (white part only)

1 red bell pepper, seeded, deribbed, and chopped

4 garlic cloves, minced

Juice of 1 lemon

4 cups chicken stock (see page 225) or canned low-salt chicken broth

1 cup low-fat plain yogurt

1 bunch fresh cilantro, stemmed

2 tablespoons ground coriander

1 teaspoon red pepper flakes

3 tablespoons minced fresh lemon thyme

Salt and freshly ground black pepper to taste

Diced Vegetable Garnish

2 tablespoons olive oil

1 zucchini, finely diced

1 yellow squash, finely diced

1 small globe eggplant, finely diced

2 tomatoes, seeded and diced

Salt and freshly ground black pepper to taste

To make the soup: Preheat the broiler. Char the eggplants on all sides in the preheated broiler. Scoop out the insides of the eggplants and discard the skin.

El Bizcocho Restaurant

In a medium saucepan over medium heat, heat the olive and sesame oil and sauté the onion, leek, red pepper, and garlic until soft, about 7 minutes. Stir in the lemon juice and eggplant and cook until the eggplant is puréed. Stir in the stock or broth and yogurt and bring the liquid to a boil. Transfer to a blender or food processor and blend until puréed. Strain through a sieve and stir in the remaining ingredients. Return to the saucepan and keep warm while preparing the garnish.

To make the garnish: In a large skillet or sauté pan over medium-high heat, heat the olive oil and sauté the vegetables until crisp-tender, about 2 or 3 minutes. Season with salt and pepper.

Ladle the soup into bowls and top with the vegetable garnish.

Makes 4 to 6 servings

Per Serving
Calories 520 • Carbohydrates 54 g • Cholesterol 5 mg
Fat 32 g • Protein 11 g • Sodium 85 mg

El Bizcocho Restaurant

Grilled Duck Breast with Oranges and Basil

⅓ cup sugar

⅓ cup unseasoned rice wine vinegar

3 tablespoons water

4 teaspoons peppercorns

1 whole clove

1 bay leaf

2 small red onions, cut into thin slices and separated into rings

1⅓ pounds duck breast with skin

Salt and freshly ground black pepper to taste

16 orange segments (see page 232)

4 teaspoons champagne vinegar

4 teaspoons orange juice

⅓ cup olive oil

8 Belgium endive leaves

2 small heads oak leaf lettuce

Salt and freshly ground black pepper to taste

1 small bunch fresh basil, preferably opal basil, stemmed and
   cut into julienne

4 teaspoons minced fresh chives

Light a fire in a charcoal grill. While the coals are heating, in a medium saucepan over high heat, combine the sugar, vinegar, water, peppercorns, cloves, and bay leaf and bring to a boil. Remove from heat and add the onion rings; set aside for at least 30 minutes.

Season the duck breast with salt and pepper. When the coals are hot, grill the duck breast, skin-side down, for 5 minutes, then turn and grill for 5 minutes on the second side. Let cool and remove the skin.

In a medium bowl, whisk together the vinegar, orange juice, and olive oil to make a vinaigrette. Toss the endive and lettuce together with a little of

El Bizcocho Restaurant

the vinaigrette until lightly coated.

Place the endive and lettuce at the top of each of 4 plates. Drain the red onion slices and mound them in the center of each plate. Thinly slice the duck breasts, arrange over the onion, and surround with orange sections. Sprinkle with the remaining vinaigrette and the basil and chives.

Makes 4 servings

Per Serving
Calories 480 • Carbohydrates 34 g • Cholesterol 75 mg
Fat 29 g • Protein 24 g • Sodium 75 mg

El Bizcocho Restaurant

Apple Tart with Cinnamon and Ginger Infusion

Start this recipe the day before serving.

Cinnamon and Ginger Infusion

1 cup sugar

⅓ cup water

2 teaspoons grated lemon zest

3 tablespoons sliced peeled fresh ginger

3 whole cloves

1 cinnamon stick

8 ounces thawed frozen puff pastry

4 Granny Smith or Pippin apples, peeled, cored, and thinly sliced

To make the infusion: In a small, heavy saucepan over high heat, bring the sugar and water to a boil and cook until it is light amber in color; watch carefully to keep it from burning. Immediately remove the caramel from heat and let cool slightly. Add the remaining ingredients, cover, and let sit for at least 8 hours. Strain.

Preheat the oven to 375°F. On a lightly floured board, roll out the puff pastry to ⅛ inch thick and cut into four 6-inch rounds. Place the pastry rounds on a baking sheet. Overlap the apple slices in a circle on top of the pastry discs and brush with the infusion. Bake in the preheated oven for 20 minutes, or until the pastry is golden brown. Remove from the oven, baste again with the infusion, and serve immediately.

Makes 4 servings

Per Serving
Calories 440 • Carbohydrates 87 g • Cholesterol 0 mg
Fat 11 g • Protein 3 g • Sodium 75 mg

El Bizcocho Restaurant

Ritz-Carlton, Chicago
The Dining Room

Chicago, Illinois

One of the finest hotels in the world, The Ritz-Carlton, Chicago, includes guest rooms and suites, four restaurants and lounges, a complete health and fitness center, and meeting salons on Chicago's North Michigan Avenue, The Magnificent Mile. This Four Seasons Regent Hotel has been honored with the highest possible accolades, including the American Automobile's Five-Diamond Award for fifteen consecutive years and recognition as Best Hotel in the United States by readers of *Traveler* magazine in 1995.

The Dining Room presents contemporary French cuisine in an elegant setting of crystal chandeliers, cozy banquettes, exquisite flowers, and performances of piano music during dinner. Chef Sarah Stegner's classical French menu marries French technique to American products, with influences from Italy and Spain and inspiration from the best possible ingredients. Chef Stegner was named Rising Star Chef of the Year by The James Beard Foundation 1995. She is a founding member of the Chicago Chef's Alliance and founded The Women Chefs of Chicago, a group that provides food for numerous local charity benefits.

The Dining Room offers Four Seasons Alternative Cuisine. Featuring health-conscious selections for gourmet tastes, Alternative Cuisine is lower in calories, cholesterol, sodium, and fat content. The Dining Room also serves a popular Sunday brunch. It was voted One of the Top Nine Hotel Dining Rooms in the United States in 1994 by *Food & Wine* magazine. For eleven consecutive years, *The Wine Spectator* has honored The Dining Room with its Grand Award for one of the top wine lists in the country. The following dinner recipes were created by chef Sarah Stegner, and the dessert recipe was created by pastry chef Sebastien Canonne.

The Dining Room

THE MENU
The Dining Room

𝄢

Tomato-Fennel Soup with Balsamic-glazed Red Onions

White and Green Asparagus Salad with Pears

Sautéed Halibut on a Bed of Oven-roasted Beets

Mint Milk Flan with Orange Water

Serves Four

Tomato-Fennel Soup with Balsamic-glazed Red Onions

This wonderful summer soup is best when made with tomatoes at the height of the season.

Balsamic-glazed Red Onions

1 small red onion, diced

2 tablespoons balsamic vinegar

1 tablespoon sugar

2 tablespoons water

1 tablespoon olive oil

12 ounces white mushrooms, stemmed and thinly sliced

1 large fennel bulb, halved, cored and very thinly sliced

1 small onion, diced

3 garlic cloves, minced

2 each large yellow and red tomatoes, peeled, seeded,
   and chopped (see page 231)

Salt and freshly cracked black pepper to taste

6 cups chicken stock (see page 225), vegetable stock,
   or canned low-salt chicken broth

Pinch of saffron

1 tablespoon fresh thyme leaves

3 ounces (3 handfuls) baby spinach, stemmed

1 tablespoon Pernod (optional)

1 tablespoon basil olive oil (see page 230)

French bread croutons, (see page 231), optional

To make the balsamic-glazed red onions: In a small saucepan over medium heat, cook the onion, vinegar, sugar, and water until the liquid reduces to a sticky glaze. Set aside.

In a large skillet or sauté pan over high heat, heat the olive oil and sauté

The Dining Room

the mushrooms, fennel, onion, garlic, and tomatoes for 5 minutes. Season with salt and pepper. Add the stock or broth and saffron. Cook to reduce the liquid by two thirds, about 20 minutes. Taste and adjust the seasoning.

Just before serving, add the thyme, spinach, and a splash of Pernod, if desired. Ladle the soup into 4 heated bowls. Sprinkle with the balsamic-glazed red onions. Top with croutons, if desired, and a drizzle of basil olive oil.

Makes 4 servings

Per Serving (without Pernod or croutons)
Calories 200 • Carbohydrates 26 g • Cholesterol 0 mg
Fat 9 g • Protein 9 g • Sodium 125 mg

The Dining Room

White and Green Asparagus Salad with Pears

24 green asparagus spears
12 white asparagus spears
2 ripe pears
¼ cup unseasoned rice wine vinegar
1 teaspoon crushed black peppercorns
2 fresh thyme sprigs
2 tablespoons olive oil
Salt to taste
4 handfuls mâche or mixed baby greens
¼ cup chopped walnuts, toasted (see page 232)

Peel the ends of the green and white asparagus spears and slice them into 3-inch lengths, then wash and drain. Boil the green asparagus for about 5 minutes, or until they are crisp-tender. Drain and immediately plunge the asparagus into a bowl of ice and water; set aside. Cook the white asparagus in boiling salted water until they are quite tender, about 6 to 8 minutes. Immediately transfer the asparagus to a bowl of ice and water.

Core, peel, and chop 1 of the pears. In a small saucepan over high heat, bring the rice wine vinegar, peppercorns, thyme, and chopped pear to a boil. Remove from heat and set aside to cool. Strain the pear-vinegar mixture through a fine-meshed sieve into a medium bowl. Stir in the olive oil until well blended. Add the white asparagus and marinate for 30 minutes before serving.

Just before serving, core and slice the remaining pear. In a medium bowl, toss together the pear slices, white asparagus and its marinade, salt, and mâche or baby greens. Fan out the green asparagus spears on each of 4 plates. Arrange the pear and asparagus salad in the center of each plate and garnish with toasted walnuts.

Makes 4 servings

Per Serving
Calories 190 • Carbohydrates 21 g • Cholesterol 5 mg
Fat 12 g • Protein 5 g • Sodium 5 mg

The Dining Room

Sautéed Halibut on a Bed of Oven-roasted Beets

2 fresh beets
5 tablespoons olive oil
1 salsify root, peeled and cut into eight crosswise slices
Four 5-ounce halibut fillets
Salt and freshly ground black pepper to taste
Juice of 1 lemon
1 tablespoon minced fresh chives

Preheat the oven to 375°F. Trim the beets, leaving 1 inch of stem. Scrub them well. Rub the beets with 1 tablespoon of the olive oil and place in a baking pan. Roast in the preheated oven until tender, about 1 to 1½ hours. Let cool, then peel and finely dice. Set aside.

Blanch the salsify pieces in boiling salted water for 2 minutes; drain. In a sauté pan or skillet over medium heat, heat 1 tablespoon of the olive oil and sauté the salsify until golden brown. Set aside.

Season the halibut fillets with salt and pepper. In a medium sauté pan over high heat, heat the remaining 3 tablespoons olive oil and sauté the halibut until golden brown on the outside and opaque throughout, about 3 minutes on each side. Remove from the pan.

In a small bowl, combine the lemon juice, diced beets, and chives. Season with salt and pepper to taste. Divide the salsify and beets onto each of 4 warmed plates. Place a halibut fillet on top of the vegetables and pour the juices from the pan on top of each fish.

Makes 4 servings

Per Serving
Calories 350 • Carbohydrates 10 g • Cholesterol 45 mg
Fat 20 g • Protein 31 g • Sodium 115 mg

The Dining Room

Mint Milk Flan with Orange Water

⅞ cup low-fat (2 percent) milk

3 tablespoons heavy (whipping) cream

1 tablespoon sugar

4 fresh mint sprigs, minced

2 tablespoons water

1 teaspoon plain gelatin

1½ cups freshly squeezed navel orange juice

Fruit Garnish

4 fresh strawberries, hulled and halved

8 fresh blueberries, halved

4 kiwis, peeled and halved

8 fresh blackberries, halved

1 small plum, sliced

1 small orange, peeled and sectioned (see page 232)

8 fresh raspberries

4 fresh gooseberries

¼ cup fresh wild strawberries (optional)

Fresh mint sprigs for garnish

In a small saucepan over medium heat, combine the milk, cream, and sugar; cook until warm. Remove from heat and add the fresh mint; cover and let steep for half an hour. Strain through a fine-meshed sieve. Place the water in a small bowl and sprinkle the gelatin over. Place the bowl over simmering water and stir until the gelatin is dissolved. Blend the dissolved gelatin into the milk mixture and pour the mixture into 4 individual soufflé dishes. Cover and refrigerate overnight.

Just before serving, strain the orange juice through a coffee filter. In a medium bowl, gently combine all the fruits for the garnish. Unmold the flans

The Dining Room

and place them in the center of each of 4 shallow soup bowls. Arrange some of the fruit around each flan and add the orange water. Garnish with mint sprigs.

Makes 4 servings

Per Serving (without wild strawberries or mint garnish)
Calories 200 • Carbohydrates 35 g • Cholesterol 20 mg
Fat 6 g • Protein 5 g • Sodium 40 mg

San Domenico NY

New York, New York

Tony May opened San Domenico NY in 1988, and the restaurant still sets the standard for modern Italian cuisine in the United States. San Domenico has received three stars from the *New York Times* for its *alta cucina,* the cooking of Italy's aristocracy, and *Esquire* magazine has called San Domenico "one of the five best restaurants in the country."

Tony May has been at the forefront of efforts in the United States and Italy to foster a more complete understanding of Italian food and wine. He is the founder of the Gruppo Ristoratori Italiani, an association of restaurateurs, chefs, writers, and food purveyors dedicated to preserving and developing Italian cooking, and the author of *Italian Cuisine: Basic Cooking Techniques,* a textbook distributed exclusively to culinary arts schools throughout America. He travels frequently to Italy to gather new ideas for the restaurant's constantly evolving menu. Tony May's restaurant career has spanned four decades, and he is included in the *Who's Who of Cooking in America.*

San Domenico NY is located across from Central Park, just two blocks north of Carnegie Hall. The dining room's sleek lines, terra-cotta colors, burnished woods, and marble floors exemplify classic Italian style and give the restaurant a light and relaxing environment.

Executive chef Theo Schoenegger hails from Northern Italy and turns out dishes that visiting Italians rave about. Diners may order the chef's *menu de gustazione,* or dine quite reasonably from fixed-price lunch and dinner menus. San Domenico NY has an extensive collection of wines from Italy, California, and the Pacific Northwest.

THE MENU
San Domenico NY

Fresh Spaghetti with Tomato and Basil Sauce

Fillets of Sea Bass in White Wine and Basil Sauce

Braised Guinea Hen with Savoy Cabbage and Porcini Mushrooms

Terrine of Warm Fruit with White Wine

Serves Two

San Domenico NY

Fresh Spaghetti with Tomato and Basil Sauce

Spaghetti
1½ cups unbleached all-purpose flour
1 tablespoon dry white wine
2 extra-large eggs
Pinch of salt

Tomato and Basil Sauce
1½ tablespoons extra-virgin olive oil
1 garlic clove, minced
1 pound tomatoes, peeled, seeded, and diced
⅓ cup lightly packed fresh basil leaves, coarsely chopped
Pinch of red pepper flakes
Salt to taste

2 teaspoons grated Parmesan cheese

Mound the flour on a large marble or wooden board and create a well in the center. Add the white wine, eggs, and salt to the well and work all the ingredients together by carefully incorporating the flour from the outside of the well. Knead for approximately 8 minutes, or until a smooth, elastic dough is achieved. Cover the dough with a cloth and let rest for 30 minutes. Roll the dough out on a lightly floured board or in a pasta machine and cut it into long, very narrow noodles.

To make the sauce: In a saucepan over medium heat, heat the olive oil and sauté the garlic for 2 minutes. Add the tomatoes, basil, pepper flakes, and salt and simmer the sauce for 20 to 25 minutes. Bring a large amount of salted water to a boil. Just before serving, cook the pasta about 2 to 3 minutes, or until al dente; drain. In a large bowl, toss together the pasta, warm tomato sauce, and Parmesan cheese; serve immediately.

Makes 2 servings

Per Serving
Calories 440 • Carbohydrates 35 g • Cholesterol 215 mg
Fat 28 g • Protein 13 g • Sodium 210 mg

San Domenico NY

Fillets of Sea Bass in White Wine and Basil Sauce

Two 8-ounce sea bass fillets
1 cup dry white wine
½ cup fish stock or bottled clam juice
¼ cup diced tomato
6 ounces potatoes, peeled and cut into julienne
Salt and freshly ground black pepper to taste
2 teaspoons extra-virgin olive oil
1½ tablespoons butter
1½ tablespoons minced fresh basil

Preheat the oven to 350°F. Place the fillets, wine, fish stock or clam juice, tomato, potatoes, salt, and pepper in a flameproof terrine or baking dish. Bake in the preheated oven for 15 minutes, or until the fillets are opaque throughout. Using a metal spatula, carefully transfer the fillets to a plate, cover, and keep warm. Place the terrine or baking dish over medium-high heat and bring the liquid to a boil; cook to reduce the liquid by half. Remove from heat and whisk in the olive oil, butter, and basil. Place a fillet in the center of each of 2 plates, spoon the sauce over, and serve immediately.

Makes 2 servings

Per Serving
Calories 470 • Carbohydrates 17 g • Cholesterol 215 mg
Fat 19 g • Protein 45 g • Sodium 270 mg

San Domenico NY

Braised Guinea Hen with Savoy Cabbage and Porcini Mushrooms

One 3-pound guinea hen, or 2 Cornish game hens
Salt and ground white pepper to taste
3 garlic cloves, chopped
1 fresh rosemary sprig, minced
6 ounces fresh porcini mushrooms, diced
1 small head Savoy cabbage, cored and coarsely chopped
2 cups beef stock or canned low-salt beef broth

Preheat the oven to 300°F. Season the hen or hens with salt and pepper and truss. Coat a baking dish with olive-oil cooking spray, add the hen or hens, and bake in the preheated oven for 1 hour, or until a meat thermometer inserted in an inner thigh registers 180°F or the juices run clear when a thigh is pierced.

Meanwhile, film a large skillet or sauté pan with olive-oil cooking spray, heat over medium heat, and sauté the garlic and rosemary for 2 or 3 minutes; do not let the garlic brown. Remove the garlic and rosemary and recoat the pan with olive-oil spray. Sauté the mushrooms over high heat for about 2 minutes. Add the cabbage leaves and beef stock or broth, reduce the heat to low, and simmer for about 30 minutes. Add salt and pepper and set aside.

When the hen or hens are done, spoon off as much fat as possible from the baking dish. Add the cabbage and porcini mixture to the pan; cover and bake for 10 more minutes. Cut the hen or hens into serving pieces and arrange them on 2 heated plates. Garnish with cabbage and porcini and serve immediately.

Makes 2 servings

Per Serving
Calories 350 • Carbohydrates 8 g • Cholesterol 130 mg
Fat 15 g • Protein 44 g • Sodium 160 mg

San Domenico NY

Terrine of Warm Fruit with White Wine

½ banana, peeled and diced
¼ pineapple, peeled, cored, and diced
4 strawberries, hulled and diced
½ pear, peeled, cored, and diced
1 orange, peeled, sectioned (see page 232), and diced
2 tablespoons sugar
½ cup dry white wine
1 sheet thawed frozen puff pastry
1 egg yolk, beaten
3 tablespoons honey, warmed

Preheat the oven to 400°F. In a large bowl, combine the fruit, sugar, and wine. Divide the mixture between 2 individual ovenproof terrines or soufflé dishes.

Roll the puff pastry out on a lightly floured board to a thickness of ¾ inch. Cut the pastry into 2 pieces the same shape as the terrines or dishes but about ¾ inch larger. Brush the edges of the puff pastry rounds with egg yolk and cover the fruit with the pastry. Seal the edges and refrigerate the terrines or dishes for about 5 minutes to chill the pastry.

Remove the terrines or dishes from the refrigerator and brush the pastry with the beaten egg yolk. Bake in the preheated oven for 15 minutes, or until the pastry is puffed and golden brown. Brush the pastry with honey and serve immediately.

Makes 2 servings

Per Serving
Calories 450 • Carbohydrates 82 g • Cholesterol 105 mg
Fat 12 g • Protein 5 g • Sodium 65 mg

San Domenico NY

The Shelburne Inn
The Shoalwater Restaurant

Seaview, Washington

The Shelburne Inn is the oldest continuously run hotel in the state of Washington. Named after the grand Shelbourne Hotel in Dublin, Ireland, it was built in 1896 by Charles Beaver. Since then the inn has been expanded several times, and today is a retreat for city dwellers and a sanctuary for nature lovers. Located between the Columbia River and the Pacific Ocean on the Long Beach Peninsula, the Shelburne is surrounded by a natural paradise complete with bird sanctuaries, lighthouses, and oyster farms. It is owned and operated by David Campiche and Laurie Anderson, who have appointed its fifteen rooms with antiques and restored its original Victorian charm. Chef David Campiche serves renowned country breakfasts family-style at the large oak table in the lobby. The breakfast menu features fresh seafood from nearby waters, local fruits and vegetables, and fresh breads and muffins baked by Laurie Anderson. Creative and delicious low-fat or vegetarian preparations are often featured, or can be made on request.

Tony and Ann Kischner's Shoalwater Restaurant, located on the Shelburne's main floor, is one of America's culinary treasures. Chef Cheri Walker's menu of Northwest cuisine emphasizes fresh, locally harvested seafood and vegetables. Oysters, mainly Pacific and Kumamoto, figure prominently on the menu, and daily-changing specials are also improvised. "In a restaurant this size," says Tony Kischner, "you can buy small quantities of seasonal rarities and use them immediately." Mouthwatering desserts are prepared by pastry chef Ann Kischner. The Shoalwater's extensive wine list emphasizes wines of the Northwest.

The Shoalwater Restaurant

THE MENU
The Shoalwater Restaurant

Bloody Mary Gazpacho

Wild Mushroom and Goat Cheese Salad with Salalberry Vinaigrette

Clams with Pesto

Pear-Sage Glazed Chicken with Kale

Rhubarb Sorbet

Serves Four

The Shoalwater Restaurant

Bloody Mary Gazpacho

3 cups ice-cold water

1 tablespoon white wine vinegar

¾ teaspoon fresh lemon juice

⅓ cup tomato juice

½ teaspoon salt

¼ teaspoon freshly ground black pepper

2 tablespoons prepared horseradish

¼ teaspoon Worcestershire sauce

1½ tablespoons vodka

3 tablespoons olive oil

¼ teaspoon Tabasco sauce

1 tomato, seeded and diced (see page 231)

¾ cup diced peeled and seeded cucumber

½ cup finely diced onion

4 fresh oregano sprigs

Freshly ground black pepper for garnish

In a large bowl, stir together all the ingredients except the oregano and pepper until well blended. Cover and chill in the refrigerator for a few hours or overnight to blend the flavors. Serve in chilled shallow soup bowls, garnished with the oregano and a sprinkling of pepper.

Makes 4 servings

Per Serving
Calories 140 • Carbohydrates 6 g • Cholesterol 0 mg
Fat 10 g • Protein 1 g • Sodium 360 mg

The Shoalwater Restaurant

Wild Mushroom and Goat Cheese Salad with Salalberry Vinaigrette

1 tablespoon olive oil
8 ounces chanterelle or other wild mushrooms, cut into ¼-inch-thick slices
Salalberry Vinaigrette (recipe follows)
4 handfuls mizuna greens or mixed baby greens
4 ounces fresh mild white goat cheese, crumbled

In a medium skillet or sauté pan over medium-high heat, heat the olive oil and sauté the mushrooms for 5 minutes. Transfer to a small bowl and toss them with a little of the salalberry vinaigrette; set aside.

In a large bowl, toss the greens with enough vinaigrette to coat and divide them equally among 4 plates. Top the greens with the chanterelles and sprinkle the goat cheese over.

Makes 4 servings

Per Serving (without salalberry vinaigrette)
Calories 150 • Carbohydrates 4 g • Cholesterol 20 mg
Fat 12 g • Protein 8 g • Sodium 170 mg

The Shoalwater Restaurant

Salalberry Vinaigrette

2 tablespoons salalberry, blueberry, or raspberry vinegar
¼ teaspoon minced garlic
1 teaspoon honey
¼ teaspoon salt
¼ teaspoon freshly ground black pepper
1 teaspoon minced fresh oregano
¼ cup olive oil
2 tablespoons canola oil

In a small bowl, whisk together the vinegar, garlic, oregano, honey, salt, and pepper. Whisk constantly while slowly adding the olive and canola oils until thickened. Store leftover vinaigrette in a covered jar in the refrigerator.

Makes about ½ cup

Per Serving
Calories 100 • Carbohydrates 2 g • Cholesterol 0 mg
Fat 10 g • Protein 0 g • Sodium 65 mg

The Shoalwater Restaurant

Clams with Pesto

Pesto

4 bunches fresh basil (2 cups packed leaves)

1 tablespoon minced garlic

¼ cup pine nuts

1½ teaspoons salt

½ cup olive oil

¾ cup (3 ounces) grated Parmesan cheese

½ cup dry white wine

½ cup dry vermouth

5 pounds littleneck clams, well scrubbed

To make the pesto: In a blender or food processor, blend the basil, garlic, pine nuts, and salt until puréed. With the motor running, pour in the olive oil in a thin stream. Stop the motor and add the cheese; pulse to just blend.

In a large saucepan over high heat, combine the wine, vermouth, and 1 cup of the pesto. Add the clams, cover, and cook until the clams open, 3 to 5 minutes. Discard any clams that do not open. Divide the clams among 4 bowls, pouring the broth over.

Makes 4 servings

Per Serving
Calories 740 • Carbohydrates 17 g • Cholesterol 165 mg
Fat 42 g • Protein 68 g • Sodium 1,410 mg

Pear-Sage Glazed Chicken with Kale

Pear-Sage Glaze

2 pears, peeled, cored, and diced

¼ cup water

1½ cups chicken stock (page 225) or canned low-salt chicken broth

¼ cup brandy

¼ cup Poire William or other pear eau-de-vie

2 tablespoons balsamic vinegar

¾ teaspoon minced fresh sage, or 2 teaspoons dried sage

1 tablespoon butter, cut into pieces

Vinaigrette

½ cup vegetable oil

¼ cup raspberry vinegar

¾ teaspoon minced fresh thyme

¼ teaspoon kosher salt

Pinch of ground allspice

4 skinless, boneless chicken breast halves

1 tablespoon canola oil

1 bunch kale, stemmed and chopped

½ red onion, thinly sliced

To make the pear-sage glaze: In a medium saucepan over low heat, cook the pears and water, covered, until the pears fall apart, about 20 minutes. Transfer to a blender or food processor, purée, and strain through a fine-meshed sieve. Set aside.

In a small saucepan over high heat, cook the stock or broth until it reduces to about ¾ cup, about 15 minutes. Combine the stock or broth, pear purée, brandy, Poire William, vinegar, and sage; set aside.

The Shoalwater Restaurant

To make the vinaigrette: In a large nonaluminum skillet or sauté pan over medium heat, whisk together the oil, raspberry vinegar, thyme, salt, and allspice; set aside.

Light a fire in a charcoal grill or preheat the broiler. Meanwhile, bring the pear-sage glaze to a boil and cook until it reduces to 1½ cups. Whisk in the butter bit by bit until the sauce thickens; remove from heat and keep warm over hot water.

When the coals are hot or the broiler heated, rub the chicken breasts with the oil, sprinkle with salt, and grill or broil on each side for about 3 minutes, or until opaque throughout. Transfer to a plate.

Return the vinaigrette to medium-high heat, add the kale and onion, and stir for a few seconds until the kale is slightly wilted; do not overcook. Divide the kale mixture among 4 warmed plates and arrange the chicken breasts on top. Spoon the pear-sage glaze over the chicken and serve immediately.

Makes 4 servings

Per Serving
Calories 580 • Carbohydrates 29 g • Cholesterol 50 mg
Fat 43 g • Protein 17 g • Sodium 250 mg

The Shoalwater Restaurant

Rhubarb Sorbet

This delicious sorbet has a lovely pink color and a creamy consistency. It can also be used as a refreshing palate cleanser between courses.

Simple Syrup
1½ cups sugar
1½ cups water

4 cups sliced fresh rhubarb
¼ cup water

To make the simple syrup: In a medium saucepan, bring the sugar and water to a full boil over high heat; remove from heat immediately. Let cool, then refrigerate until chilled.

Preheat the oven to 350°F. In a baking dish, place the rhubarb and water. Cover with aluminum foil and bake for 45 minutes, or until the rhubarb is soft but still holds its shape. Let cool, then refrigerate until chilled.

Add the chilled syrup and rhubarb to an ice cream maker and freeze according to manufacturer's instructions. Serve the rhubarb sorbet the same day it is made.

Makes 1½ quarts

Per Serving
Calories 110 • Carbohydrates 27 g • Cholesterol 0 mg
Fat 0 g • Protein 0 g • Sodium 0 mg

The Shoalwater Restaurant

Stein Ericksen Lodge
Glitretind Restaurant

Park City, Utah

Named for Olympic gold medalist Stein Ericksen, Deer Valley Resort's director of skiing, The Stein Ericksen Lodge offers European charm, luxurious accommodations, warm service, country comfort, and some of the most beautiful scenery in the Wasatch Mountains. Lodge guests enjoy ski-in, ski-out access to the slopes, a year-round heated swimming pool, a sauna, a hot tub, a fitness room, massage therapy, mountain biking, hiking, and summer festivals.

The Stein Ericksen Lodge has been awarded the Mobil Travel Guide Four-Star Award and the *Traveler* magazine Readers' Choice Award as the Best Mainland Resort of 1992. Stein Ericksen Lodge is a member of the prestigious Small Luxury Hotels of the World and Relais & Chateaux.

The Glitretind Restaurant serves contemporary American-Continental cuisine. An excellent Sunday brunch is accompanied by live jazz music. The wine list has consistently received *The Wine Spectator* Award of Excellence. In the summer, guests enjoy fabulous mountain views from a dining deck. The following menu and recipes were created by David Derfel.

THE MENU
Glitretind Restaurant

Fennel and Leek Vichyssoise with Fresh Chives

Cholesterol-Free Caesar Salad

Baked Halibut with Fresh Ginger and Lemongrass Broth

Low-Fat Chocolate-Raspberry Crème Brûlée

Serves Two

Fennel and Leek Vichyssoise with Fresh Chives

1 tablespoon olive oil

1 cup chopped fennel

1 cup chopped leek (white part only)

4 cups water

1 potato, peeled and diced

¼ teaspoon minced fresh thyme

½ cup non-fat plain yogurt

1 teaspoon salt

½ teaspoon freshly ground black pepper

1 teaspoon minced fresh chives

In a medium saucepan over medium heat, heat the olive oil and sauté the fennel and leek until the leek is translucent, about 5 minutes. Add the water, potato, and thyme; reduce the heat to low and cook for 10 minutes. Transfer the soup to a blender or food processor and pureé. Strain the soup through a sieve into a bowl, cover, and refrigerate until completely chilled.

Just before serving, whisk in the yogurt, season with salt and pepper, and sprinkle with chives.

Makes 4 servings

Per Serving
Calories 95 • Carbohydrates 13 g • Cholesterol 0 mg
Fat 3.5 g • Protein 3 g • Sodium 580 mg

Glitretind Restaurant

Cholesterol-Free Caesar Salad

½ egg white

¼ cup extra-virgin olive oil

1 tablespoon water

1 teaspoon minced garlic

¼ teaspoon Dijon mustard

¼ teaspoon salt

Freshly ground black pepper to taste

1 head romaine lettuce, rinsed, dried, and torn into pieces

¾ cup baked croutons (see page 231)

1 teaspoon cracked pepper

Place the egg white in a medium bowl and whisk in the olive oil in a thin stream. Gradually whisk in the water, then the garlic, mustard, salt, and pepper.

Remove the outer leaves of the romaine until reaching the pale green inner leaves; rinse, dry, and tear into pieces. In a medium bowl, toss together the romaine, the dressing, and croutons; sprinkle with cracked pepper.

Make 2 servings

Per Serving
Calories 330 • Carbohydrates 12 g • Cholesterol 0 mg
Fat 29 g • Protein 4 g • Sodium 385 mg

Glitretind Restaurant

Baked Halibut with Fresh Ginger and Lemongrass Broth

Two 5-ounce halibut fillets
Salt and freshly ground black pepper to taste
1 cup water
2 teaspoons minced fresh ginger
2 teaspoons minced lemongrass
1 teaspoon salt
2 tablespoons diced green onions (white part only)
2 tablespoons diced, peeled, and seeded tomato
½ teaspoon freshly ground black pepper

Preheat the oven to 400°F. Sprinkle the halibut fillets with salt and pepper. Spray a baking dish with vegetable-oil cooking spray and add the halibut and water. Bake in the preheated oven for 7 to 8 minutes, or until the fish is opaque throughout. Strain the liquid in the baking dish into a small saucepan. Add the ginger and lemongrass and simmer gently for 5 minutes. Add the remaining ingredients. Arrange the halibut fillets on 2 plates and spoon the broth over.

Makes 2 servings

Per Serving
Calories 180 • Carbohydrates 3 g • Cholesterol 50 mg
Fat 4 g • Protein 28 g • Sodium 1,190 mg

Glitretind Restaurant

Low-Fat Chocolate-Raspberry Crème Brûlée

1 cup low-fat (2 percent) milk
½ teaspoon vanilla extract
2 teaspoons unsweetened cocoa powder
¼ cup plus 1 tablespoon packed brown sugar
2 egg whites
½ cup fresh raspberries

Preheat the oven to 300°F. In a medium bowl, whisk together the milk, vanilla, cocoa, and the ¼ cup brown sugar, then blend in the egg whites.

Divide the raspberries between two 1-cup ovenproof molds and pour in the milk mixture. Place the molds in a baking dish and pour warm water into the dish to halfway up the sides of the molds. Bake in the preheated oven for 45 minutes, or just until set. Refrigerate for several hours, or until thoroughly chilled.

Just before serving, preheat the broiler. Place the 1 tablespoon brown sugar in a fine-meshed sieve and push half of it through with the back of a spoon to evenly layer the top of each custard. Place the custards under the broiler about 2 inches from the heat until the sugar is melted and crisp, about 20 seconds, being careful not to burn it. Let cool for a few minutes and serve.

Makes 2 servings

Per Serving
Calories 230 • Carbohydrates 44 g • Cholesterol 10 mg
Fat 3 g • Protein 8 g • Sodium 130 mg

Terra

St. Helena, California

Terra is an extraordinary restaurant set in the heart of Napa Valley, California's world-famous wine country. When Lissa Doumani and Hiro Sone launched the restaurant in 1988, they wanted to create a romantic setting with a comfortable atmosphere. Their numerous awards include the DiRoNa Award in 1994 and the Distinguished Restaurant Award by *Traveler* magazine in 1992 and 1993.

Terra's two dining rooms occupy the ground floor of St. Helena's historic Hatchery Building. Built as a foundry in 1884, the two-story structure is now listed in the National Register of Historic Places. The flowers and paintings in Terra's dining rooms contrast with heavy beams and rugged fieldstone walls.

Chef Hiro Sone's menu changes with the seasons and mingles flavors from Asia, Northern Italy, and Southern France. Emphasizing olive oil and fresh herbs, and using such Asian ingredients as basmati rice, Thai curry, ponzu, and miso sauces, Sone's cuisine is one of unexpected but satisfying flavor combinations. After training at the prestigious cooking school, École Technique Hôtelière Tsuji, in Osaka, Hiro met Lissa when both worked at Spago in Los Angeles. Hiro was preparing himself for the position of sous chef at Spago's new Tokyo branch and Lissa was a pastry cook. True to their restaurant's wine-country locale, Lissa and Hiro feature local wines on their well-rounded list. They select only one label from each winery, in order to highlight as many local vintners as possible. Terra's wine list has been given the Award of Excellence by *The Wine Spectator*. The following recipes were created by Hiro Sone.

THE MENU

Terra

Blood Orange and Fennel Salad

Pistou Soup with Goat Cheese Ravioli

Grilled Swordfish and Rigatoni with Tomato, Caper, and Black Olive Sauce

Pomegranate Granita

Serves Four

Blood Orange and Fennel Salad

A salad with a wonderful balance of textures, colors, and tastes.

1 small fennel bulb
4 blood oranges
2 teaspoons balsamic vinegar
3 tablespoons extra-virgin olive oil
Salt and freshly ground black pepper to taste
1 small tomato, seeded and diced
4 handfuls mixed baby greens
Julienned zest of 1 blood orange for garnish

Slice the bottom and top off the fennel bulb and remove the tough outer leaves. Quarter the bulb, cut out the core, and slice the bulb as thinly as possible. Peel the oranges, removing all the pith, and cut them into crosswise slices.

In a small bowl, whisk together the vinegar, olive oil, salt, and pepper to make a vinaigrette.

In a medium bowl, toss together the fennel, tomato, and baby greens with half of the vinaigrette. Mound the salad in the center of each of 4 plates. Arrange the orange slices around the salad and sprinkle them with the remaining vinaigrette. Top with a sprinkling of orange zest and pepper.

Makes 4 servings

Per Serving
Calories 190 • Carbohydrates 24 g • Cholesterol 0 mg
Fat 11 g • Protein 3 g • Sodium 45 mg

Terra

Pistou Soup with Goat Cheese Ravioli

Pistou

1 tablespoon minced garlic

½ cup packed fresh basil leaves

½ cup packed fresh parsley leaves

¼ to ½ cup extra-virgin olive oil

¼ cup diced seeded tomato

Salt and freshly ground black pepper to taste

Soup

2 tablespoons olive oil

½ cup finely diced onion

1 tablespoon minced garlic

½ cup finely diced carrot

½ cup finely diced celery

½ cup finely diced red bell pepper

½ cup finely diced turnip

½ cup finely diced leeks

½ cup finely diced zucchini

½ cup finely diced eggplant

½ tablespoon minced fresh oregano

4 cups chicken stock (see page 225) or canned low-salt chicken broth

1 cup tomato purée

2 cups cooked white beans

Salt and freshly ground black pepper to taste

12 Goat Cheese Ravioli (recipe follows)

Parmesan cheese for sprinkling

To make the pistou: In a blender or food processor, purée all of the ingredients. Cover and set aside.

To make the soup: In a large saucepan over medium heat, heat the olive oil and sauté the onion and garlic until light brown. Add the diced vegetables and oregano and sauté until the vegetables are soft. Add the stock or broth, tomato purée, and beans and bring to a boil, skimming any foam that rises to the surface. Reduce the heat to low and simmer for about 3 minutes. Season with salt and pepper.

Meanwhile, bring a large pot of salted water to a boil. Drop in the ravioli and cook until they rise to the surface, about 2 to 3 minutes; drain.

Add the pistou to the hot soup. Divide the ravioli among 4 or 6 shallow soup bowls and ladle the soup over. Sprinkle the soup with Parmesan cheese and serve.

Makes 4 to 6 servings

Per Serving (without Parmesan cheese)
Calories 510 • Carbohydrates 47 g • Cholesterol 60 mg
Fat 26 g • Protein 23 g • Sodium 670 mg

Goat Cheese Ravioli

8 ounces fresh goat cheese at room temperature
6 tablespoons grated Parmesan cheese
1 egg yolk
Pinch of ground white pepper
1 egg white
½ cup water
24 wonton wrappers

In a medium bowl, mix the goat cheese, Parmesan, egg yolk, and white pepper until thoroughly blended; set aside.

In a small bowl, mix together the egg white and water. Place the goat cheese mixture in a pastry bag and pipe about 1 tablespoon onto the center

Terra

of each of 12 wonton wrappers. Brush the edges of all the wonton wrappers with the egg wash, lay a wonton wrapper on top of the cheese mixture, and close by pressing together lightly.

Makes 12 ravioli; serves 4

Per Serving (without Parmesan cheese)
Calories 120 • Carbohydrates 10 g • Cholesterol 30 mg
Fat 6 g • Protein 7 g • Sodium 230 mg

Grilled Swordfish and Rigatoni with Tomato, Caper, and Black Olive Sauce

Tomato, Caper, and Black Olive Sauce

3 teaspoons olive oil

3 garlic cloves, minced

1 pinch red pepper flakes

1 small onion, chopped

5 large tomatoes, peeled, seeded, and chopped (see page 231)

1 cup chicken stock (see page 225) or canned low-salt chicken broth

18 Niçoise olives, pitted

1 tablespoon capers, drained

Salt and freshly ground black pepper to taste

⅓ cup dried bread crumbs

2 tablespoons grated Parmesan cheese

2 teaspoons minced fresh parsley

1 garlic clove, minced

Four 1-inch-thick swordfish steaks (about 4 ounces each)

1 teaspoon olive oil

2 teaspoons Dijon mustard

6 ounces rigatoni

1 tablespoon minced fresh basil

Light a fire in a charcoal grill. While the coals are heating, make the sauce: In a heavy saucepan over medium heat, heat the olive oil and sauté the garlic and pepper flakes for 2 to 3 minutes, until lightly browned. Add the onion and sauté until lightly browned, about 7 minutes. Add the tomatoes and stock or broth and simmer for 5 minutes. Remove from heat and stir in the remaining ingredients. Set aside and keep warm.

In a blender or food processor, blend the bread crumbs, Parmesan cheese, parsley, and garlic together. Set aside.

Just before grilling the fish, bring a large pot of salted water to a boil.

While the coals are heating, brush the swordfish steaks with the olive oil and place them, oiled-side down, on the grill over very hot coals. Grill until opaque on the outside but slightly translucent in the center, about 4 minutes on each side. Transfer from the grill to a broiler pan and brush evenly with mustard. Preheat the broiler.

Cook the pasta in the boiling water until al dente, about 10 minutes; drain.

Sprinkle the bread crumb mixture over each fish steak and broil the steaks for 30 seconds, or until golden brown on top. In a large bowl, mix together the sauce, rigatoni, and fresh basil. Mound some of the pasta in the center of each of 4 warmed plates and top with a broiled swordfish steak.

Makes 4 servings

Per Serving
Calories 450 • Carbohydrates 46 g • Cholesterol 45 mg
Fat 15 g • Protein 33 g • Sodium 810 mg

Terra

Pomegranate Granita

Granita has a coarser, more granular texture than sorbet because it is frozen in a pan and stirred occasionally.

6 large pomegranates
⅔ cup fresh orange juice
1 tablespoon fresh lemon juice
⅓ cup sugar

Cut the pomegranates in half crosswise and juice with an orange juicer. You should have 3 cups of juice. (Take care, as pomegranate juice stains.) In a medium bowl, stir together the pomegranate juice, orange juice, lemon juice, and sugar. Pour into a stainless steel pan and place in the freezer for about 30 minutes. Remove from the freezer and stir gently. Return the pan to the freezer, stirring every 30 minutes for 3 to 4 hours, or until the mixture is the texture of crushed ice. (Do not allow the juice mixture to freeze completely.) Serve the granita in chilled martini glasses.

Makes 4 servings

Per Serving
Calories 170 • Carbohydrates 43 g • Cholesterol 0 mg
Fat 0 g • Protein less than 1 g • Sodium 0 mg

Terra

Terra Ristorante Italiano

Greenwich, Connecticut

In 1991 Ramze Zakka opened Terra Ristorante Italiano in a setting that combines the informal atmosphere of a Tuscan country home with the stylishness of an urbane, see-and-be-seen gathering place. Located in central Greenwich, the restaurant's rustic dining rooms are highlighted by half-barrel ceilings with painted canvas frescoes. Two terraces provide delightful alfresco dining when the weather permits.

Chef Albert DeAngelis's menu is elegant in its simplicity and has a firm Tuscan foundation. A wood-fired grill and oven maximize the inherent flavors of the ingredients without adding fat or calories. The constantly changing menu offers inventive pizzas and a full range of pastas, fresh fish, and meats. The following menu and recipes were created by chef Albert DeAngelis.

Terra Ristorante Italiano

THE MENU
Terra Ristorante Italiano

♪

Warm Goat Cheese with Grilled Eggplant and Balsamic Vinaigrette

Tuscan Seafood and Bean Soup

Grilled Squab with Green Lentils, Prosciutto, and Balsamic Vinegar

Hazelnut-Orange Polenta Cake with Berries and Yogurt

Serves Four

Terra Ristorante Italiano

Warm Goat Cheese with Grilled Eggplant and Balsamic Vinaigrette

6 tablespoons olive oil, plus more for drizzling
2 tablespoons balsamic vinegar
1 globe eggplant, cut into ¼-inch-thick slices
10 fresh basil leaves, minced
10 fresh parsley sprigs, minced
Salt and freshly ground black pepper to taste
4 Tuscan bread slices, crusts removed
One 4-ounce log fresh white goat cheese
¼ cup pine nuts
2 handfuls mixed baby greens

Light a fire in a charcoal grill. While the coals are heating, in a medium bowl, whisk together the 6 tablespoons of olive oil and balsamic vinegar to make a vinaigrette. Place the eggplant slices in a single layer in a large shallow glass baking dish and spoon half of the vinaigrette over, reserving the remaining vinaigrette. Sprinkle with the basil, parsley, salt, and pepper and set aside to marinate.

When the coals are hot, grill the eggplant for 3 minutes on each side, or until golden brown. Set aside.

Meanwhile, preheat the oven to 400°F and lightly coat a baking sheet with olive oil. Cut the bread into diamond shapes about 2 inches wide and 3 inches long. Slice the goat cheese into ½-inch-thick slices and layer 3 slices of cheese on top of each piece of bread. Press some pine nuts into the cheese and drizzle with a little olive oil. Arrange on the prepared baking sheet and bake in the preheated oven for about 10 minutes, or until the bread is toasted and the goat cheese melted.

In a medium bowl, toss the baby greens with the reserved vinaigrette. Place the greens in the center of a platter and surround them with grilled

Terra Ristorante Italiano

eggplant slices and goat cheese croutons.

Makes 8 croutons; serves 4 as an appetizer

Per Serving
Calories 420• Carbohydrates 27 g • Cholesterol 15 mg
Fat 33 g • Protein 10 g • Sodium 280 mg

Tuscan Seafood and Bean Soup

½ cup dried cannellini or Great Northern beans

3 tablespoons olive oil

1 onion, diced

2 garlic cloves, minced

½ fennel bulb, diced

2 carrots, peeled and diced

2 celery stalks, diced

2 tomatoes, chopped

1 bay leaf

2 fresh thyme sprigs

Pinch of saffron

4 cups fish stock or bottled clam juice

8 mussels

4 ounces cockles or baby clams

4 medium shrimp, shelled and deveined

4 bay scallops, rinsed and patted dry

½ cup dry white wine

5 basil leaves, finely chopped

10 fresh parsley sprigs, finely chopped

Salt and freshly ground black pepper to taste

Rinse and pick through the beans. Place them in a bowl, cover with cold water, and soak overnight; drain and set aside.

In a large, heavy pot over medium heat, heat 2 tablespoons of the olive oil and sauté the onion and garlic until translucent, about 7 minutes. Add the fennel, carrots, and celery and sauté for 5 minutes. Add the beans, tomatoes, bay leaf, thyme, saffron, and fish stock or clam juice. Raise the heat to high and bring to a boil. Reduce the heat to low and simmer, stirring occasionally, until the beans are tender, about 1 hour.

Just before cooking the shellfish, scrub the mussels and cockles or baby

Terra Ristorante Italiano

clams well and debeard the mussels. In a shallow saucepan over medium heat, heat the the remaining 1 tablespoon olive oil and sauté the shrimp and scallops for 2 minutes. Add the mussels and cockles or baby clams. Add the white wine to the pan, stir to scrape up any browned bits on the bottom of the pan, cover, and cook until the mussels and clams open, about 5 minutes. Discard any mussels or clams that do not open. Add the shellfish and wine to the soup. Add the basil, parsley, salt, and pepper to the soup and serve.

Makes 4 servings

Note: The mussel and clam shells should be tightly closed. To store them before cooking, place them in a bowl with water to cover and 1 teaspoon salt.

Per Serving
Calories 410 • Carbohydrates 34 g • Cholesterol 100 mg
Fat 14 g • Protein 35 g • Sodium 410 mg

Terra Ristorante Italiano

Grilled Squab with Green Lentils, Prosciutto, and Balsamic Vinegar

2 cups French green lentils

3 tablespoons olive oil

1 onion, finely chopped

3 garlic cloves, minced

2 carrots, peeled and finely diced

3 celery stalks, finely diced

2 ounces prosciutto, diced

¼ cup dry white wine

2 cups chicken stock (see page 225), vegetable stock (see page 228), or canned low-salt chicken broth, heated

½ teaspoon ground cumin

1 bay leaf

10 fresh basil leaves, minced

10 fresh parsley sprigs, minced

Salt and freshly ground black pepper to taste

Four 1-pound squab or Cornish hens

1 handful mixed baby greens

2 teaspoons Herb Vinaigrette (see page 57)

½ tablespoon aged balsamic vinegar

Blanch the lentils in salted boiling water for 4 minutes; drain and set aside.

In a large saucepan over medium heat, heat 2 tablespoons of the olive oil and sauté the onion, garlic, carrots, celery, and prosciutto for 3 minutes. Add the lentils, pour in the white wine, and stir to scrape up any browned bits on the bottom of the pan. Cook to reduce the liquid by half. Gradually add the stock or broth and cook for 20 to 30 minutes, or until the lentils are tender. Add the cumin, bay leaf, basil, parsley, salt, and pepper. Set aside.

Light a charcoal fire in a grill. Remove the breasts from the squab or Cornish hens, leaving the wing bone intact. Remove the thighs and legs in one piece. Drizzle with the remaining 1 tablespoon olive oil and season with salt and pepper.

When the coals are hot, grill the squab or Cornish hens, skin-side down, for 5 minutes. Turn and grill for 5 minutes on the second side. The breasts should be opaque throughout but still slightly pink, and the legs and thighs should be fully cooked. Transfer to a baking pan, loosely cover with aluminum foil, and let sit.

Heat the lentils. In a small bowl, toss the baby greens with the vinaigrette. Place the lentils in the center of a large platter. Arrange the squabs or hens around the lentils and top each with a little of the baby greens. Drizzle the balsamic vinegar over the squab or hens and lentils and serve.

Makes 4 servings

Per Serving

Calories 920 • Carbohydrates 64 g • Cholesterol 160 mg
Fat 38 g • Protein 81 g • Sodium 1,160 mg

Terra Ristorante Italiano

Hazelnut-Orange Polenta Cake with Berries and Yogurt

1 cup (5 ounces) hazelnuts, toasted, peeled,
   and finely chopped (see page 232)
1 cup yellow cornmeal
¼ cup unbleached all-purpose flour
½ cup sugar
½ cup (1 stick) butter, at room temperature
1 tablespoon minced orange zest
½ cup fresh strawberries, hulled and halved
½ cup fresh raspberries
½ cup fresh blueberries
2 tablespoons Grand Marnier
1 cup low-fat plain yogurt

Preheat the oven to 400°F. Butter a 9-inch springform pan.

In a blender or food processor, combine the hazelnuts, cornmeal, flour, sugar, butter, and orange zest. Process until just combined. Press the mixture evenly and firmly into the prepared pan and bake in the preheated oven for 25 minutes. Let cool slightly and unmold.

Meanwhile, in a medium bowl, gently combine the strawberries, raspberries, blueberries, and Grand Marnier. Fold in the yogurt.

Place a slice of warm cake on each of 4 warmed plates, top with the yogurt and berries, and serve at once.

Makes one 9-inch single-layer cake; serves 8

Per Serving
Calories 380 • Carbohydrates 38 g • Cholesterol 35 mg
Fat 24 g • Protein 6 g • Sodium 140 mg

Terra Ristorante Italiano

Windsor Court Hotel
The Grill Room

New Orleans, Louisiana

The Grill Room of the Windsor Court Hotel in New Orleans is modeled after the famed Grill in London's Savoy Hotel. A Lalique table stands at the entrance, and the focus point of the elegant room is a marquetry screen of Windsor Castle especially created for the hotel.

In a city known for spectacular food, The Grill Room is acclaimed for its New Orleans Grande Cuisine, a blend of classic French cuisine with contemporary international influences. A few of its accolades include recognition as the only American Automobile Association Five Diamond Restaurant in New Orleans and one of *Food & Wine's* Top Twenty-five Restaurants in America.

The Grill Room's menu is seasonal and changes daily. Classical French techniques are used to create innovative variations on standard dishes that bring out individual ingredient flavors, textures, and colors. The menu is complemented by a fine wine cellar. The following menu and recipes were created by chef Kevin Graham.

THE MENU
The Grill Room

Bayoubaisse

White Bean and Lentil Salad

Steam-roasted Grouper with Herb Tea

Sweet Risotto with Grilled Pineapple and Mango

Serves Four

Bayoubaisse

After years of making the classic bouillabaisse from Provence, chef Graham has adapted the recipe to use fish and shellfish native to southeastern Louisiana. Almost any combination of shellfish, such as lobsters, crabs, and mussels and firm-fleshed fish, such as snapper and grouper, is delicious in this hearty soup.

Infused Fish Stock

1 tablespoon extra-virgin olive oil

½ fennel bulb, finely shredded

1 tablespoon tomato paste

2 oranges, peeled and cut into quarters

1 lemon, halved

6 cups Fish Stock (see page 227)

4 tablespoons extra-virgin olive oil

Four 2-ounce red drum or white sea bass fillets

8 ounces medium shrimp, peeled and deveined

Four 2-ounce grouper or black sea bass or cod fillets

1 onion, finely chopped

1 leek (white part only) finely chopped

2 garlic cloves, crushed

Pinch of saffron threads

1 tablespoon minced fresh parsley

1 small bay leaf

¼ teaspoon minced fresh savory

¼ teaspoon fennel seeds

1 tomato, peeled, seeded, and chopped

8 small new potatoes, peeled and halved

1 carrot, peeled and shredded

4 ounces fresh lump crabmeat, picked over to remove
   any shell and cartilage

4 ounces crayfish, peeled

8 oysters, shucked
Salt and freshly ground black pepper to taste
Fresh croutons (see page 231)

To make the infused fish stock: In a large saucepan over medium-high heat, heat the oil until it begins to sizzle. Add the fennel and sauté until soft, about 5 minutes. Stir in the tomato paste and cook for 2 minutes. Add the remaining ingredients, reduce the heat to low, and simmer for 15 minutes. Remove from heat, strain through a sieve, and let cool to room temperature.

In a large saucepan over high heat, heat 2 tablespoons of the olive oil until it just starts to smoke. Add the red drum or white sea bass fillets and sear for about 30 seconds on each side. Remove from the pan with a metal spatula and drain on paper towels. Add the shrimp to the pan and sear, tossing frequently, for about 1 minute. Remove the shrimp with a slotted spoon. Add the grouper or black sea bass or cod fillets to the pan and sear for about 30 seconds on each side. Remove the fish from the pan with a metal spatula.

In the same pot over high heat, heat the remaining 2 tablespoons of the olive oil and sauté the onion, leek, garlic, saffron, parsley, bay leaf, savory, and fennel seeds until the onion is translucent, about 5 minutes. Add the tomato and cook until it softens and breaks apart; add the potatoes, carrot, and infused fish stock. Bring the liquid to a boil, then reduce the heat to low and simmer for 15 minutes. Return the fish and shrimp to the pot and simmer for 2 minutes; do not overcook. Remove the pot from the heat and gently fold in the crab and crayfish. Season with salt and pepper.

Just before serving, place 1 or 2 oysters in the center of each bowl and spoon the fish, shrimp, and stock over the oysters. Serve with fresh croutons.

Makes 4 to 6 servings

Per Serving (with stock but without croutons)
Calories 600 • Carbohydrates 57 g • Cholesterol 140 mg
Fat 25 g • Protein 36 g • Sodium 600 mg

The Grill Room

White Bean and Lentil Salad

This salad may be made in advance, covered, and refrigerated. Let it sit at room temperature for 1 hour before serving.

White Beans

1 cup dried navy beans

4 cups chicken stock (see page 225) or canned low-salt chicken broth

1 cup minced onion

½ teaspoon ground white pepper

¼ teaspoon red pepper flakes

1 garlic clove, minced

1 bay leaf

Salt to taste

Lentils

1 cup lentils, rinsed

3 cups chicken stock (see page 225) or canned low-salt
  chicken broth, or more as needed

¼ cup minced onion

1 garlic clove, minced

1 bay leaf

3 fresh parsley sprigs

1 large onion, minced

1 teaspoon roasted garlic purée (see page 231)

2 tomatoes, peeled, seeded, and finely diced (see page 231)

1 tablespoon capers, drained

1 teaspooon minced fresh oregano

2 tablespoons cider vinegar

2 tablespoons extra-virgin olive oil

½ teaspoon cracked black pepper

Cayenne pepper and salt to taste

The Grill Room

Pick through the beans and discard any pebbles or broken or discolored beans. Place the beans in a large saucepan and cover with water. Remove any beans that float to the surface; soak the beans overnight. Or, in a large saucepan over high heat, combine the beans and water to cover. Bring the liquid to a boil and cook for 2 minutes. Remove from heat, cover, and let stand for 1 hour.

Drain the beans and return to the saucepan. Add the stock or broth, minced onion, white pepper, pepper flakes, garlic, and bay leaf. Bring the beans to a slow boil, reduce the heat, cover, and simmer until tender, 1 to 1½ hours. Drain the beans, discard the bay leaf, add salt, and let cool to room temperature.

In a large saucepan over high heat, combine the lentils, stock or broth, onion, garlic, bay leaf, and parsley sprigs. Bring the liquid to a boil, cover and reduce the heat, and simmer for about 45 to 60 minutes, or until the lentils are tender. Stir occasionally and add more stock or broth, if necessary. Remove from heat, drain any excess broth, discard the bay leaf and parsley, and let cool to room temperature.

In a large bowl, stir together the white beans, lentils, minced onion, roasted garlic purée, tomatoes, capers, oregano, vinegar, oil, and pepper. Add cayenne and salt and serve at room temperature.

Makes 4 servings

Per Serving
Calories 500 • Carbohydrates 73 g • Cholesterol 0 mg
Fat 10 g • Protein 33 g • Sodium 200 mg

The Grill Room

Steam-roasted Grouper with Herb Tea

This versatile recipe can be adapted to black sea bass or cod and can be served either warm or cold. In Asia, tea is considered an aid to digestion and accompanies every meal. Borrowing from that tradition, this steam-roasted grouper is served with a homemade tea extracted from commonly available herbs.

¼ cup vegetable oil

Four 8-ounce grouper (preferably scamp grouper), black sea bass, or
   cod fillets, with skin

Salt and freshly ground black pepper to taste

½ cup finely sliced onion

2 cups shredded Napa cabbage, bok choy, or Savoy cabbage

3 ounces shiitake mushrooms, stemmed and finely diced

1 bay leaf

Pinch of caraway seeds

¼ cup dry white wine

Minced fresh flat-leaf (Italian) parsley for garnish

Herb Tea (recipe follows)

Preheat the oven to 450°F. In a large, heavy, ovenproof skillet over high heat, heat the vegetable oil to just below the smoking point. Season the fish with salt and pepper. Place the fillets, flesh-side down, in the hot oil for a few seconds. Turn and sear the skin side for 1 minute. Remove the fish from the pan and set aside. Add the onion, cabbage or bok choy, mushrooms, bay leaf, and caraway seeds to the pan. Lower the heat to medium and cook until tender, about 7 minutes. Drain and discard any liquid. Stir in the white wine.

In the same large skillet, place the fish fillets on top of the cabbage or bok choy mixture. Cover the pan tightly with aluminum foil and place in the preheated oven for 5 minutes, or until the fish flakes when tested with a fork. Remove the fish from the pan. Drain off any excess liquid from the cabbage or bok choy mixture, toss, and adjust the seasoning with salt and pepper, if necessary.

Place a fish fillet in the center of each plate. Spoon some of the cabbage or bok choy mixture around the fish and garnish with parsley. Serve with herb tea.

Makes 4 servings

Per Serving (without herb tea)
Calories 360 • Carbohydrates 7 g • Cholesterol 85 mg
Fat 16 g • Protein 45 g • Sodium 130 mg

The Grill Room

Herb Tea

¾ cup lightly packed fresh basil leaves
¾ cup lightly packed fresh mint leaves
¾ cup lightly packed fresh dill
¼ cup honey, plus more if needed
4 cups water, boiling

In a heatproof pitcher, combine the basil, mint, and dill. Add the ¼ cup honey and pour in the water. Let steep for 10 minutes. Serve hot or over ice. Sweeten with additional honey, if desired.

Makes 4 servings

Per Serving
Calories 360 • Carbohydrates 7 g • Cholesterol 85 mg
Fat 16 g • Protein 45 g • Sodium 130 mg

The Grill Room

Sweet Risotto with Grilled Pineapple and Mango

Chopped nuts or dried fruit may be added to the rice, and a dollop of Marscapone cheese may be used to garnish each serving.

2 mangoes
½ cup Arborio rice
2 cups low-fat (1 percent) milk
¼ cup sugar
2 tablespoons unsalted butter (optional)
1 vanilla bean, split lengthwise
1 egg yolk (optional)
1 pineapple, peeled, cored and cut into ½-inch slices

Light a fire in a charcoal grill. While the coals are heating, prepare the fruit and risotto.

To slice the mangoes, hold one upright on a cutting board, with the thick base of the fruit down. With a sharp knife, cut off 1 lengthwise side of the fruit close to the pit. Repeat on the other 3 sides. Holding 1 section of fruit skin-side down on a cutting board, make a series of criss-cross incisions into the flesh to cut a diamond pattern into the fruit without cutting all the way through the mango skin. Repeat with the remaining mango section and set aside.

Place the rice in a fine-meshed sieve and rinse under cold running water for 2 minutes; drain.

In a heavy saucepan over medium-high heat, combine the milk, sugar, optional butter, and vanilla bean. Bring the liquid to a slow boil and add the rice. Reduce the heat and simmer gently, stirring continuously, for about 15 minutes, or until the rice is al dente. Add the egg yolk, if desired, to thicken and give the risotto a creamier texture. Remove the pan from heat, remove the vanilla bean, and cover the saucepan to keep warm.

The Grill Room

When the coals are hot, place the pineapple slices on the grill until the grill marks are definite, about 3 to 5 minutes on each side. Transfer the pineapple slices to a plate and keep warm. Place the mango slices on the grill, flesh-side down, for no longer than 2 to 3 minutes. Transfer to a plate.

Scoop the risotto into 4 serving bowls and arrange the grilled fruit on plates around the bowls. Serve immediately.

Makes 4 servings

Per Serving
Calories 320 • Carbohydrates 70 g • Cholesterol 5 mg
Fat 2 g • Protein 7 g • Sodium 65 mg

Zenzero

Santa Monica, California

Kazuto Matsusaka opened his glamorous Pacific Rim restaurant in 1993 to immediate acclaim. Born and raised in Japan, Kazuto moved to California at the age of twenty-three and gained experience working as a chef in traditional French and Japanese kitchens. As the longtime chef at Wolfgang Puck's Chinois on Main, Kazuto enjoyed a collaboration with Puck that spanned over ten years.

Zenzero's highly designed contemporary dining room is strikingly beautiful. A glass front wall silhouettes palm trees and the setting sun against the Pacific sky. The light, airy dining room provides a serene environment that complements Kazuto's artfully presented menu of simple, elegant food. Although Kazuto eventually decided against his original menu concept of blending Asian and Italian cuisine, he kept the name Zenzero, which means "ginger" in Italian.

Inspired by the cuisines of Asia and France, Kazuto's inventive dishes are brought out one at a time and placed in the center of the table so everyone can taste them. The family-style service encourages many to make a meal of shared starter dishes. Zenzero's wine list is a connoisseur's selection of affordable all-California wines. Guided by an East-meets-West philosophy and his playful enthusiasm for food, Kazuto creates exceptional food at Zenzero.

THE MENU

Zenzero

Sautéed Wild Mushroom Salad

Chinese Green Onion Soup

Assorted Baby Lettuces with Ponzu Dressing

Wok-seared Rice Cakes with Stir-fried Vegetables

Roasted Figs in Crushed Mulberry Sauce

Serves Two

Zenzero

Sautéed Wild Mushroom Salad

½ English cucumber, cut into fine matchsticks
½ tablespoon extra-virgin olive oil
½ teaspoon peanut oil
1 cup (3 ounces) diced Portobello mushroom
½ cup (1½ ounces) diced stemmed shiitake mushrooms
½ cup (1½ ounces) diced oyster mushrooms
2 tablespoons balsamic vinegar
1 cup lightly packed stemmed watercress
Salt and freshly ground black pepper to taste

In a medium bowl, toss together the cucumber and olive oil until lightly coated. Place a nest of cucumber in the center of each of 2 plates.

In a large skillet or sauté pan over high heat, heat the peanut oil until it just begins to smoke. Add the mushrooms and sauté for about 2 minutes, or until they begin to soften. Pour the balsamic vinegar around the edge of the pan so it quickly reduces and glazes the mushrooms. Quickly stir in the watercress. Season with salt and pepper. Arrange the mushrooms on top of the cucumber nests and serve immediately.

Makes 2 servings

Per Serving
Calories 100 • Carbohydrates 13 g • Cholesterol 0 mg
Fat 5 g • Protein 3 g • Sodium 10 mg

Zenzero

Chinese Green Onion Soup

1½ ounces ground chicken or turkey breast

½ small carrot, peeled and thinly sliced

½ small celery stalk, thinly sliced

¼ onion, thinly sliced

7 green onions with tops, cut into very thin slices

1 tablespoon mushroom soy sauce (available in Asian markets)

2 egg whites, lightly beaten

4 cups chicken stock (see page 225) or canned low-salt chicken broth

2 white cabbage leaves, cut into shreds

2 red cabbage leaves, cut into shreds

In a medium bowl, stir together the ground chicken or turkey, carrot, celery, onion, half of the sliced green onions, mushroom soy sauce, and egg whites until thoroughly combined.

In a stockpot over high heat, heat the stock or broth to a boil. Lower the heat to a simmer, stir the chicken or turkey mixture into the broth, and let the liquid return to a simmer. The egg will coagulate and hold the chicken or turkey mixture together in a raft. The soup should just bubble through the raft; make sure it doesn't break the raft apart. Simmer for 1 hour, then carefully strain through a fine-meshed sieve.

In a medium bowl, mix together the cabbages and the remaining sliced green onions. Ladle the soup into 2 bowls, add the cabbage mixture, and serve immediately.

Makes 4 servings

Per Serving
Calories 80 • Carbohydrates 7 g • Cholesterol 10 mg
Fat 2.5 g • Protein 9 g • Sodium 350 mg

Zenzero

Assorted Baby Lettuces with Ponzu Dressing

2½ tablespoons Ponzu Dressing (recipe follows)
⅓ cup peanut oil
¼ teaspoon chili oil
Pinch of freshly ground black pepper
4 handfuls mixed baby lettuces

In a large bowl, whisk together the dressing, oils, and pepper. Add the salad greens and toss.

Makes 2 servings

Per Serving (With ponzu dressing)
Calories 360 • Carbohydrates 7 g • Cholesterol 0 mg
Fat 36 g • Protein 2 g • Sodium 460 mg

Ponzu Dressing

This dressing is also delicious drizzled over fish.

¼ cup mirin
2 tablespoons fresh lemon juice
2 tablespoons unseasoned rice wine vinegar
2 tablespoons dark soy sauce (available in Asian markets)

In a small saucepan over high heat, bring the mirin to a boil to burn off the alcohol. Stir in the lemon juice, rice vinegar, and soy sauce and return to a boil. Remove from heat, strain through a fine-meshed sieve, and chill before using.

Makes about ½ cup

Per Serving
Calories 20 • Carbohydrates 3 g • Cholesterol 0 mg
Fat 0 g • Protein 0 g • Sodium 350 mg

Wok-seared Rice Cakes with Stir-fried Vegetables

⅓ cup short-grain white rice
¼ teaspoon sugar
½ teaspoon dark soy sauce
½ small bunch garlic chives, minced
Pinch of salt and freshly ground black pepper
1 tablespoon peanut oil
Stir-fried Vegetables (recipe follows)
Balsamic vinegar for sprinkling

Place the rice in a small saucepan and cover the rice with cold water; pour off the water. Repeat 3 times. Add cold water to the pan to cover the rice by ¾ inch. Let stand for 4 hours. Cook over high heat, uncovered, until the water and any bubbles have disappeared from the surface. Cover, reduce the heat to low, and cook for about 30 minutes, or until tender.

Meanwhile, line 4 custard cups or individual soufflé molds with plastic wrap.

In a medium bowl, combine the warm sticky rice with the sugar, soy sauce, chives, salt, and pepper. Press this rice mixture into the prepared cups or dishes.

In a wok, medium nonstick skillet, or medium sauté pan over high heat, heat the peanut oil until almost smoking. Unmold the rice cakes and carefully drop them into the hot oil. When the rice cakes start to turn golden brown, about 5 minutes, turn them and cook on the other side until golden.

Serve the rice cakes at once with the stir-fried vegetables and sprinkle with a little balsamic vinegar.

Makes 2 servings

Per Serving (without stir-fried vegetables)
Calories 360 • Carbohydrates 7 g • Cholesterol 0 mg
Fat 36 g • Protein 2 g • Sodium 460 mg

Zenzero

Stir-fried Vegetables

½ tablespoon peanut oil
½ cup broccoli florets
¼ cup halved snow peas
¼ cup asparagus tips
¼ cup diced red bell peppers
¼ cup diced yellow bell peppers
½ cup roughly chopped bok choy
¼ cup roughly chopped Japanese eggplant
¼ cup sliced red onion
1 tablespoon dark soy sauce
Salt and freshly ground black pepper to taste
½ teaspoon chili oil

In a wok, large skillet, or sauté pan over high heat, heat the peanut oil until almost smoking. Reduce the heat to medium high, add all the vegetables, and sauté just until crisp-tender. Stir in the remaining ingredients and serve immediately.

Per Serving
Calories 80 • Carbohydrates 9 g • Cholesterol 0 mg
Fat 5 g • Protein 3 g • Sodium 630 mg

Zenzero

Roasted Figs in Crushed Mulberry Sauce

Choose very ripe figs that are almost bursting and seeping a little juice. This dish is also very nice served with some vanilla ice cream or frozen yogurt.

1 cup fresh mulberries, loganberries, or blackberries
1 to 3 tablespoons sugar
4 black Mission or California figs, quartered
Juice of ½ lime

Preheat the broiler. In a small bowl, crush the berries and ½ to 1 tablespoon sugar with a fork. The amount of sugar will depend on the sweetness of the berries.

In another small bowl, combine the figs with 1 or 2 tablespoons sugar. Arrange the figs, cut-side up, on an oiled ovenproof plate. Broil the figs just until the sugar begins to caramelize, about 30 seconds. Remove from the broiler and squeeze the lime juice over the figs.

Arrange the figs attractively on 2 plates and surround with the berry sauce.

Makes 2 servings

Per Serving
Calories 130 • Carbohydrates 33 g • Cholesterol 0 mg
Fat 5 g • Protein 2 g • Sodium 10 mg

BASICS

Brown Chicken Stock

2 pounds chicken parts (backs and necks), bones, and trimmings
¾ cup *each* finely chopped carrots, onions and celery root
2 fresh rosemary sprigs
1 teaspoon tomato paste
¾ cup diced ripe tomatoes
3 quarts water

Preheat the oven to 350°F. In a baking pan, roast the chicken parts, bones and trimmings, stirring occasionally, until they are a deep brown, about 30 minutes. Add the carrots, onions, celery root, and rosemary. Continue roasting for another 4 to 5 minutes. Combine the tomato paste and diced tomatoes and mix this into the bones and vegetables. Roast another 5 to 7 minutes, being careful to avoid scorching.

Remove the baking pan from the oven and transfer all the ingredients to a large saucepan over high heat. Add 2 cups of the water and bring to a boil; cook to reduce to a glaze. Add another 2 cups of the water and cook to reduce again. Add the remaining 2 quarts water and simmer uncovered for 1 hour, skimming occasionally to remove any fat. Strain through cheesecloth or a fine-meshed sieve. Let cool. Cover and store in the refrigerator for up to 3 days or freeze for up to 2 months. To refrigerate longer, bring the stock to a boil every 3 days.

Makes 3 quarts

Chicken Stock

4 pounds chicken parts (backs and necks) and trimmings
2 onions, chopped
4 celery stalks, chopped

225

2 leeks (white part only) chopped
1 bay leaf
10 white peppercorns
1 fresh thyme sprig
1 garlic clove, chopped
1 gallon cold water

In a large stockpot, combine all of the ingredients. Bring to a boil, skimming any foam that forms on the surface. Lower the heat and simmer, uncovered, for 1 hour, skimming occasionally. Remove from heat and skim the surface one final time. Strain through a fine-meshed sieve and let cool to room temperature. Store for up to 3 days in a covered container in the refrigerator or freeze for up to 2 months.

Makes 4 quarts

Court Bouillon

4 cups water
8 parsley sprigs
4 celery leaves
2 bay leaf
½ teaspoon freshly ground black pepper
Generous pinch of fennel seed or aniseed
1 small onion, cut into quarters
1 cup dry white wine, or ¼ cup fresh lemon juice

In a large saucepan, bring all the ingredients to a boil and simmer for 20 minutes. Remove from heat and strain through a fine-meshed sieve. Let cool. Cover and refrigerate for up to 5 days.

Makes about 4 cups

Basics

Fish Stock

This stock calls for cold-water fish parts because cold-water fish are far less oily than their warm-water counterparts, thus they will not cloud the stock.

¼ cup vegetable oil
4 pounds cold-water fish heads, bones, and trimmings
   (such as sole, turbot, halibut, or whiting), washed and cut into pieces
2 onions, finely chopped
1 small bunch celery, finely chopped
1 bunch fresh parsley, chopped
2 leeks (white part only) chopped
2 bay leaves
1 fresh thyme sprig
2 cups dry white wine
4 quarts cold water

In a large stockpot over high heat, heat the oil until almost smoking. Add the fish parts, onions, celery, parsley, leeks, bay leaves, and thyme and sauté until the onions are translucent, about 5 minutes. Remove from heat, cover, and let sit for 10 minutes. Return the pot to high heat and add the wine and cold water. Bring the liquid to a boil and skim any foam that rises to the surface. Reduce the heat to medium and simmer for 30 minutes. Remove the stock from heat and skim the surface one final time. Strain through a sieve and let cool to room temperature. Store in a covered container in the refrigerator for up to 2 days or freeze for up to 2 months. To refrigerate longer, bring the stock to a boil every 2 days.

Makes 4 quarts

Veal Stock

2 pounds sliced veal shanks
2 tablespoons oil

1 onion, chopped
1 carrot, peeled and chopped
1 celery stalk, chopped
½ cup dry white wine
Salt and freshly ground pepper to taste

Preheat the oven to 400 F. In a roasting pan, toss the shanks with the oil and vegetables. Brown for 30 to 40 minutes, turning occasionally. Transfer the shanks and vegetables to a large saucepan or kettle.

Pour the fat out of the roasting pan, and place the pan over medium heat. Add the wine and cook for 2 or 3 minutes, stirring to scrape up the browned juices on the bottom of the pan. Pour this liquid into the saucepan with the bones and vegetables. Add water to cover the ingredients by 1 inch. Bring to a boil and skim off any foam that rises to the top. Add salt and pepper, cover, and simmer for 3 to 4 hours.

Strain through a sieve into a bowl and refrigerate. Remove any congealed fat that rises to the surface. Store for 3 days in a covered container in the refrigerator or freeze for up to 2 months. To keep longer in the refrigerator, bring to a boil every 3 days.

Makes about 1 quart

Vegetable Stock

2 carrots, peeled and chopped
2 celery stalks, chopped
1 green bell pepper, seeded, deribbed, and chopped
2 zucchini, chopped
1 small onion, chopped
6 ounces green beans, chopped
1 leek, chopped
1 parsnip, peeled and chopped
1 bunch spinach, stemmed

Basics

4 fresh dill sprigs
1 bay leaf
2 garlic cloves
1 teaspoon salt
1 teaspoon freshly ground black pepper
3 quarts water

In a large kettle, combine all the ingredients and bring to a boil. Reduce the heat and simmer, uncovered, for 30 minutes. Remove from heat and let sit for 30 minutes. Strain through a sieve, pressing out the liquid from the vegetables with the back of a large spoon; discard the vegetables. Return to heat and simmer for 30 minutes. Let cool. Store in a covered container in the refrigerator for 3 to 4 days, or freeze for up to 2 months.

Makes about 6 cups

Apricot Sauce

4 fresh apricots, halved, pitted, and diced
½ cup water
2 tablespoons sugar

In a medium, heavy saucepan over high heat, combine the apricots, water, and sugar and bring to a boil. Lower the heat and cook gently until the apricots are soft, about 5 minutes. Remove from heat and transfer to a blender or food processor and purée.

Return the purée to the saucepan and bring to a boil. Lower the heat and simmer for 5 minutes. Transfer to a bowl and let the apricot sauce cool before using. Apricot sauce may be stored in a covered container in the refrigerator for up to 3 days.

Basics

Pesto

1 cup chopped fresh basil leaves
1 garlic clove
⅓ cup extra-virgin olive oil
½ ounce pine nuts
2 tablespoons grated Parmesan cheese

In a blender or food processor, purée all of the ingredients to make a smooth sauce. Cover and refrigerate for up to 3 days.

Makes about ½ cup

Basil Olive Oil

3 fresh basil sprigs
1 cup good-quality olive oil

Push the basil into a half-pint glass container and add the olive oil. Place in a dark place for a couple of months to let the flavors develop. Strain through double layers of cheesecloth or a fine-meshed sieve before use.

Clarified Butter

In a heavy saucepan, melt unsalted butter over low heat until it bubbles. Remove the pan from heat and carefully skim off the foamy butterfat that has risen to the surface. Pour the clear yellow liquid into a container, leaving the milky residue at the bottom; cover. Clarified butter will keep for months in the refrigerator or freezer.

Croutons

4 slices French bread, about ½ inch thick
1 garlic clove, halved
1 tablespoon extra-virgin olive oil

Preheat the broiler. Arrange the bread slices in a single layer on a baking sheet and place under the broiler for 2 to 3 minutes, or until toasted. Remove from heat, rub with the garlic cloves, and brush with olive oil on both sides. Return to the broiler and toast on the other side. Serve immediately, or let cool and store in an airtight container for up to 1 week.

Makes about 2 cups

Roasted Garlic

1 whole garlic bulb
Extra-virgin olive oil for brushing

Preheat the oven to 350°F. Using a sharp knife, trim the roots from the garlic head and cut off the top of the bulb, exposing the individual garlic cloves. Place the bulb root-side-down in a shallow baking pan. Brush or rub the garlic bulb with olive oil and wrap in aluminum foil. Seal tightly and place in the preheated oven for 1 ½ hours. Let cool. Unwrap the garlic and squeeze out the pulp.

Peeling and Seeding Tomatoes

Remove the core from the tomatoes and cut an X in the opposite end. Drop the tomatoes into a pot of rapidly boiling water for 3 to 4 seconds, or until the skin by the X peels away slightly. Plunge the tomatoes into a bowl of cold water; the skin should slip off easily. To seed, cut the tomatoes in half crosswise, hold each half upside down over the sink, and gently squeeze and shake to remove the seeds.

Roasting and Peeling Peppers

Char peppers over a gas flame or under a preheated broiler until the skin is blackened all over. Using tongs, transfer the peppers to a paper or plastic bag, close it, and let the peppers cool for 10 to 15 minutes. Remove from the bag, peel off the skins with your fingers or a small sharp knife, and core and seed the peppers.

To Section Citrus Fruit

Cut off the top and bottom of an orange, grapefruit, lime, or lemon down to the flesh, then stand the fruit upright and cut off the peel in sections down to the flesh. Working over a bowl to catch the juice, hold the fruit in one hand and cut between the membranes. Rotate the fruit and let the sections fall into the bowl. Pick out any seeds.

Toasting Nuts

Preheat the oven to 350°F. Spread the nuts on a baking sheet or jelly roll pan and bake for 5 to 8 minutes or until fragrant and lightly toasted, stirring once or twice. Whole roasted nuts may be stored in an airtight container in the refrigerator or freezer.

Toasting and Peeling Hazelnuts

Preheat the oven to 350°F. Spread the nuts on a baking sheet or in a jelly-roll pan and bake for 10 to 15 minutes or until lightly browned, stirring once or twice. Remove from the oven, fold in a kitchen towel, and let cool for 5 minutes. Rub the hazelnuts with the towel to remove the skins. Pour the nuts into a colander and shake it over the sink to discard remaining skins.

CONVERSION CHARTS

Weight Measurements

Standard U.S.	Ounces	Metric
1 ounce	1	30 g
¼ lb	4	125 g
½ lb	8	250 g
1 lb	16	500 g
1½ lb	24	750 g
2 lb	32	1 kg
2½ lb	40	1.25 kg
3 lb	48	1.5 kg

Volume Measurements

Standard U.S.	Ounces	Metric
1 T	½	15 ml
2 T	1	30 ml
3 T	1½	45 ml
¼ cup (4 T)	2	60 ml
6 T	3	90 ml
½ cup (8 T)	4	125 ml
1 cup	8	250 ml
1 pint (2 cups)	16	500 ml
4 cups	32	1 L

Oven Temperatures

Fahrenheit	Celsius
300°	150°
325°	165°
350°	180°
375°	190°
400°	200°
425°	220°
450°	230°

Conversion Factors

Ounces to grams: Multiply the ounce figure by 28.3 to get the number of grams.

Pounds to grams: Multiply the pound figure by 453.59 to get the number of grams.

Pounds to kilograms: Multiply the pound figure by 0.45 to get the number of kilograms.

Ounces to milliliters: Multiply the ounce figure by 30 to get the number of milliliters.

Cups to liters: Multiply the cup figure by 0.24 to get the number of liters.

Fahrenheit to Celsius: Subtract 32 from the Fahrenheit figure, multiply by 5, then divide by 9 to get the Celsius figure.

LIST OF RESTAURANTS

Brava Terrace
3010 St. Helena
Highway North
St. Helena, CA 94574
(707) 963-9300

Cafe Allegro
1815 West 39th
Kansas City, MO 64111
(816) 561-3663

Carbo's Cafe
3717 Roswell Road
Atlanta, GA 30342
(404) 231-4162

**Centro Grill and
Wine Bar**
2472 Yonge Street
Toronto, Ontario
Canada M4P 2H5
(416) 483-2211

Chanterelles
1312 Spruce Street
Philadelphia, PA 19107
(215) 735-7551

Chef Allen's
19088 N.E. 29th Avenue
Aventura, FL 33180
(305) 935-2900

Classic Kitchen
610 Hannibal Street
Noblesville, IN 46060
(317) 773-7385

Ernie's
847 Montgomery Street
San Francisco, CA 94133
(415) 397-5969

Four Seasons Hotel
Chartwell Restaurant
791 West Georgia Street
Vancouver, B.C.
Canada V6C 2T4
(604) 689-9333

Le Chardonnay
8284 Melrose Ave.
Los Angeles, CA 90046
(213) 655-8880

New World Grill
329 West 49th Street
New York, NY 10019
(212) 957-4745

Oritalia
1915 Fillmore Street
San Francisco, CA 94115
(415) 346-1333

The Peaks at Telluride
The Legends of Telluride
136 Country Club Drive
Telluride, CO 81435
(303) 728-6800

Quadrangle Grille
2800 Routh, Suite 180
Dallas, TX 75201
(214) 979-9022

**Quail Lodge Resort &
Golf Club**
The Covey Restaurant
8205 Valley Greens Dr.
Carmel, CA 93923
(408) 624-1581

Rancho Bernardo Inn
El Bizcocho Restaurant
17550 Bernardo Oaks Drive
San Diego, CA 92128
(619) 487-1611

The Ritz-Carlton Hotel
The Dining Room
160 East Pearson Street
Chicago, IL 60611
(312) 266-1000

San Domenico
240 Central Park South
New York, NY 10019
(212) 265-5959

Shelburne Inn
The Shoalwater Restaurant
4415 Pacific Way
Seaview, WA 98644
(206) 642-2442

Stein Eriksen Lodge
Post Office Box 3177
Park City, UT 84060
(801) 649-3700

Terra
1345 Railroad Avenue
St. Helena, CA 94574
(707) 963-1234

Terra Ristorante
156 Greenwich Avenue
Greenwich, CT 06830
(203) 629-5222

Windsor Court Hotel
Grill Room
300 Gravier Street
New Orleans, LA 70130
(504) 523-6000

Zenzero
1535 Ocean Avenue
Santa Monica, CA 90401
(310) 451-4455

List of Restaurants

ACKNOWLEDGMENTS

I would like to thank the many people who made this volume possible.

I am forever grateful to Dick Hindman, an incredible musician, for allowing me to record his original compositions. My thanks to Mike Cogan of Bay Records for excellence as recording engineer and for production supervision. Once again, thanks to George Horn for the digital mastering.

My deepest gratitude to the proprietors and chefs of the restaurants who generously contributed menus and recipes to the cookbook: Fred Halpert, Stephen Cole, Stu Stein, Carmen and Bob Mazurek, Tony Longo, Marc Thuet, Philippe Chin, Allen Susser, Steven Keneipp, Terry Fischer, David Kinch, Marc Miron, Robert Bigonnet, Claude Alrivy, Katy Keck, Richard Barber, Nori Yoshida, Bruce Hill, Rick Houston, Robert Kowalske, Tom Stark, Wayne Reynolds, Csaba Ajan, Bob Williamson, Rushton Hays, Thomas Dowling, Nicholas Mutton, Sarah Stegner, Sebastien Canonne, Tony May, Theo Schoenegger, David Campiche, Laurie Anderson, Tony and Ann Kischner, Richard Erb, David Derfel, Hiro Sone, Lissa Doumani, Ramze Zakka, Albert DeAngelis, Daniel Mann, Kevin Graham, and Kazuto Matsusaka. And thanks go to the staffs of the restaurants for their prompt assistance.

Once again, thanks to my editor Carolyn Miller for her expert guidance and meticulous attention to detail. I also owe many thanks to Steve Patterson, Jim Armstrong, Ned Waring, and Eric Liebau for numerous contributions, and to the rest of the staff at Menus and Music. Karen Duester deserves thanks for her gracious help, as does Bruce Nalezny at the Piedmont Piano Company for his kind assistance.

My most sincere thanks to Tom Kamegai for his wonderful drawings and design, and thanks again to Michael Osborne for his design, good advice, and enthusiastic support of this project. As always, to my daughters Claire and Caitlin and my husband John for their adventurous appetites and their love.

Acknowledgments

INDEX

Index

Index

Index

Index

Index

Index

Scott Sibley

Sharon O'Connor is a musician, author, and cook. She also is the founder of the San Francisco String Quartet and creator of the Menus and Music series, which combines her love of music and food. Lighthearted Gourmet is the ninth volume in her series of cookbooks with musical recordings.